Words Their Way™

Letter and Picture Sorts for Emergent Spellers

Second Edition

Donald R. Bear
University of Nevada, Reno

Francine Johnston
University of North Carolina at Greensboro

Marcia Invernizzi
University of Virginia

Shane Templeton
University of Nevada, Reno

Allyn & Bacon

Boston   New York   San Francisco
Mexico City   Montreal   Toronto   London   Madrid   Munich   Paris
Hong Kong   Singapore   Tokyo   Cape Town   Sydney

Executive Editor: *Linda Ashe Bishop*
Development Editor: *Hope Madden*
Series Editorial Assistant: *Jacqueline Gillen*
Executive Marketing Manager: *Krista Clark*
Production Editor: *Annette Joseph*
Editorial Production Service: *Omegatype Typography, Inc.*
Composition Buyer: *Linda Cox*
Manufacturing Manager: *Megan Cochran*
Electronic Composition: *Omegatype Typography, Inc.*
Illustrator: *Francine Johnston*
Cover Administrator: *Linda Knowles*

For Professional Development resources, visit www.allynbaconmerrill.com.

Between the time website information is gathered and then published, it is not unusual for some sites to have closed. Also, the transcription of URLs can result in typographical errors. The publisher would appreciate notification where these errors occur so that they may be corrected in subsequent editions.

Printed in the United States of America

10   9   8   7   BRR   13   12

Quoted content appearing on pages 86 and 93 is reprinted with the permission of Simon and Schuster Books for Young Readers, an imprint of Simon & Schuster Children's Publishing Division, from *Chicka Chicka Boom Boom* by Bill Martin Jr. and John Archambault. Text copyright © 1989 Bill Martin Jr. and John Archambault.

Allyn & Bacon
is an imprint of

www.pearsonhighered.com

ISBN-10:   0-13-514579-1
ISBN-13:   978-0-13-514579-1

Contents

Overview

Words Their Way: Letter and Picture Sorts for Emergent Spellers is intended to complement Words Their Way: Word Study for Phonics, Vocabulary, and Spelling Instruction. That core text describes a practical, research-based, and classroom-proven way to study words with students. This companion text provides materials, sorts, and activities specifically for emergent word study. It is important that teachers have the core text available for reference as it provides the theory and research for the activities in this book. Chapter 4 of Words Their Way: Word Study for Phonics, Vocabulary, and Spelling Instruction (or Words Their Way, as we shall refer to it hereafter) describes word study for emergent learners in detail and suggests additional activities.

Words Their Way: Letter and Picture Sorts for Emergent Spellers provides teachers with prepared reproducible sorts and step-by-step directions to guide students through the sorting lessons. There are organizational tips as well as follow-up activities to extend the lesson through weekly routines. The materials provided in this text will complement the use of any existing phonics, spelling, and reading curricula.

Emergent learners are found mostly in preschool, kindergarten, and the beginning of first grade. They may not write at all or they might write with scribbles, letter-like forms, or random letters. If students are using letters to represent the initial sounds of words (spelling cat as K or baby as BB) they are moving into the early letter name–alphabetic stage, but will still benefit from many of the activities in this book. Emergent learners cannot read in the conventional sense, but can follow along in simple predictable text with the support of memory and pictures, and it is from such pretend reading that they begin to develop a concept of word.

SCOPE OF THIS BOOK

Chapter 1 in this supplement provides a variety of assessments for children in the emergent stage. These assessments help you determine what students know and don't know and what instruction to plan for them. The following chapters cover concept sorts, phonological awareness, alphabet knowledge, beginning consonant sounds, and concept of word.

Chapter 2's concept sorts are a good place to begin, because students can learn the process of sorting using familiar objects and ideas while they extend their thinking and vocabulary. Phonemic awareness, rhyming, syllabication, and sound play are described in Chapter 3 and complement the study of alphabet knowledge and letter recognition described in Chapter 4. Chapter 5 introduces the systematic study of beginning consonants through explicit instruction using sound sorts. Finally, Chapter 6 focuses on concept of word in print, but poems, jingles, and other short text selections are included in all chapters to read with students and to use in word study activities.

THE INTEGRATED LITERACY DIET
FOR EMERGENT LEARNERS

Though this book is organized by chapters, the chapters are not meant to be sequential as they are in the other supplemental texts. Concept sorts are appropriate for students at all ages because they introduce and reinforce vocabulary and conceptual knowledge. Reading selections are provided with the concept sorts and alphabet and phonological awareness activities so that emergent learners are interacting with print right from the start. Kindergarten students can begin to sort by sounds at the same time they are learning to identify letters and track a line of print. Once students have a concept of word, they begin to collect sight words they have learned to read in familiar texts. Such is the integrated literary diet for the emergent learner.

Chapters 2 through 6 incorporate units designed to show you how all these elements can be integrated and revisited throughout the emergent stage. We hope these models will help you create your own integrated literacy experiences using the materials in this book as well as favorite materials from your classroom. The sequence of instruction can be modified by teachers to fit the sequence in their own core reading program and should be differentiated to meet the needs of their students.

Word study activities are integrated into five essential literacy activities: Read To, Read With, Write With, Word Study, and Talk With (RRWWT). The following chart describes these essential activities.

Essential Literacy Activities	Procedures and Activities
Read To Concept, Vocabulary, and Language Learning	*Read To* students from literature that offers rich oral language and that involves students in discussions as in directed listening thinking activities (DLTAs). Vocabulary instruction has greater meaning when supported by what we read to students.
Read With Concept of Word in Print and Word Recognition	*Read With* students using the support of familiar, predictable, and rhyming texts. Students fingerpoint read to track brief and familiar texts on charts and in personal readers. Students match and arrange word cards and sentence strips.
Write With Phonological Awareness, Letter–Sound Correspondences, Verbal Expression, Concepts of Print, and Language Development	*Write With* activities encourage students to analyze the speech stream. Students learn to segment words for individual letter–sound correspondences as the teacher models through think-alouds and shares the pen.
Word Study Phonological Awareness, Word and Letter Recognition, Initial Sound Correspondences, Concept and Language Development, Word Learning	*Word Study* includes picture sorts to teach beginning sounds, letter sorts and cards to teach the alphabet and letter recognition, concept sorts for thinking and vocabulary instruction, rhyming and syllabication activities, and language play with rhymes and songs.
Talk With Language and Vocabulary Learning	*Talk With* students to help their oral language grow. Creative dramatics, storytelling, and talking about meaningful things make it possible for vocabulary, language structures, and thinking to mature.

PACING

Instruction in this supplement is set at an introductory, average pace. There is a year of activities, though most students will progress through these sorts in less than a year.

Make adjustments in the pacing to assure that students master the sorts. If students catch on quickly, move to a faster pace, perhaps by spending fewer days on a series of activities or by skipping some altogether. On the other hand, pacing can be slowed by using additional activities when students need more practice. *Words Their Way* provides background information, more sorts and activities, organizational tips, games, and resources that are essential to organize your word study program for emergent readers and spellers.

RESOURCES

For each chapter there are Notes for the Teacher and routines to develop the different parts of the literary diet. We provide a variety of blackline reproducible sorts to cut apart for use over several days. There are also blacklines of reading selections that students can use for fingerpoint reading. Make your own copy of the reproducibles for teacher modeling in small groups or make transparencies to use when demonstrating on an overhead projector. The pages can also be enlarged to use in pocket charts. Sorting and game templates and additional sorts are found in the Appendix of *Words Their Way* and on the *Words Their Way* CD-ROM.

For independent or small-group work, make copies of the handouts for each student, enlarging the original to eliminate the border and to increase the size of the words and pictures. Children should be taught how to cut out their own set of sorts (developing fine-motor skills in the process), but volunteers, parents, and cross-age tutors can help to prepare materials in advance to save instructional time. Sorting pieces are stored in envelopes or plastic bags that have been labeled with children's names to sort again several times on other days or to take home. Chapter 3 in *Words Their Way* includes additional ideas for managing picture sorts.

Many teachers have students from diverse language backgrounds who are learning to read in English. Throughout this book, suggestions are provided for English Learners (ELs). You will also find additional information in *Words Their Way with English Learners* and the supplement *Words Their Way: Emergent Sorts for Spanish-Speaking English Learners*.

THE WORD STUDY LESSON

The four steps in a teacher-directed lesson are discussed in Chapter 3 of *Words Their Way*. Take your time to introduce each of these four steps: *Demonstrate, Sort and Check, Reflect,* and *Extend*.

1. *Demonstrate.* Demonstrate the sorts and activities in small groups at a table, on the floor, on an overhead, or with a pocket chart. Name the pictures with students, and have students say the names of the pictures aloud with you. Listen for the pictures that students know. The pictures can be used to extend children's vocabulary by talking briefly about new terms. However, do not make naming the pictures into a guessing game. Give the words as needed or eliminate unknown items from the sort.

   Use two or three key pictures at the top of each column to establish categories. Name the picture on a card and then check it with the key pictures. ("Does *baby* go with *ball* or *monkey*? Listen—*baby–ball* or *baby–monkey*? I am going to put the picture of the baby underneath the picture of the ball because these two words sound alike at the beginning.")

   Sort each picture in this way and place them underneath the key pictures. Go slowly as you demonstrate, and explain how pictures are alike or different.

This explanation helps students learn specialized vocabulary that describes the categories; for example, *letters, sounds, rhyming,* and so on. Students sort by naming the pictures *aloud.* Saying the words together enhances student involvement, and the articulation provides essential information needed to sort by sound.

2. *Sort and Check.* Students repeat the sort individually or with a partner, or they can contribute to a whole-group sort. Pairing English-speaking children with English language learners will provide assistance with new vocabulary. For independent sorting, have students set up their own key pictures. With a partner or in the group, students can take turns drawing a card and sorting pictures in the correct column.

   Demonstrate how students are to *check* after sorting by naming the pictures in each column. Simply say, "Let's check to see if there are any pictures we might need to move." Show students how to recognize an error and move the picture to the correct column.

3. *Reflect.* Bring the group together to have students reflect on why they sorted the way they did, or talk to individuals as you move around to check their work. Common phrases you can use in reflection are "These pictures are alike because . . ." or "I sorted these pictures in this column under the _____ because . . ." There are only so many ways to complete an easy sort, so assure students that it is all right to say the same things that you or someone else did as long as it makes sense. Reflections can be written down by the teacher and collected on a bulletin board or chart. As in most learning, children will need to see the reflection process modeled by the teacher. A reflection, for example, might be "I sorted these pictures underneath the picture of the cake because they all have the same sound at the end."

4. *Extend.* Students extend their experience with the sort in many ways. At the outset, students repeat the sort independently and then extend the sort by finding more examples, hunting for similar pictures, and playing games. Over several days, students repeat these sorts in a group, for seatwork, with a partner, at centers, or for homework. Routines are described in each chapter of this book that will extend the sorts and involve students in related literacy activities.

WEEKLY SCHEDULES IN EMERGENT WORD STUDY

Daily literacy instruction blends brief lessons that occur throughout the day and are repeated over time. We suggest a weeklong routine that has students practice these essential activities to mastery. Each lesson incorporates a mix of activities in a number of essential areas: concept and vocabulary development, concept of word in print, phonological awareness, alphabet knowledge, and beginning consonant sounds. The teacher-directed lessons incorporate different components of this basic word study diet for the emergent learner.

Five days of word study can be divided into three segments, as shown in the following chart. The first two days provide crucial and explicit instruction through teacher modeling and discussion. On the remaining days, students work more independently, with repeated practice of the sorts. The Read With activities are introduced on Day 1 or Day 2, and this makes it possible to do word hunts and other word and letter recognition activities on Days 3 through 5.

Day 1	Day 2	Days 3–5
Read To: Literature Connection	Read With: Reread selections	Read To: Literature Connection
Read With: Easy selections	Word Study: Repeat sort, check and reflect	Read With: Reread familiar selections
Word Study: Demonstrate and sort, check and reflect	Extend at seats or centers	Word Study: Repeated practice with sort, word hunts, games
		Talk With and Write With

Most Read To and Read With activities can be presented in a large group setting. Differentiation then follows based on students' needs. If you work with instructional groups, Day 1 can be staggered. In addition, Days 3 to 5 can be reduced or expanded.

Chapter 1 Assessments for the Emergent Stage

NOTES FOR THE TEACHER

This chapter provides you with a variety of tools to assess your students in the emergent stage. These assessments, which complement the ongoing assessment you do as you observe students daily, can be used as pre-assessments or post-assessments, as well as to group students, to monitor growth, and to guide instruction. We describe alphabet assessments, including alphabet tracking, recitation, and recognition; phonological assessments, including rhyme and alliteration; letter–sound assessments, including beginning consonant sounds, observations of students' writing, and a spelling inventory appropriate for kindergarten students and other emergent learners; and concept of word assessments, including various forms of word recognition. Refer to the page numbers given with each assessment to find the necessary blackline masters.

In a number of instances, benchmark scores, which are based on the *Phonological Awareness Literacy Screening for Kindergartners (PALS-K)* (Invernizzi, Juel, Swank, & Meier, 2007), are reported for alphabet knowledge, phonological awareness, spelling, and concept of word. These benchmark measures from PALS have been tested on a very large sampling of children and have been found to be reliable and valid (http://pals.virginia.edu).

ALPHABET ASSESSMENTS

Alphabet Recitation and Tracking

Teach the alphabet song to preschoolers and kindergartners and sing it often. Slow it down and model pointing to the letters on a chart as it is sung. Observe to see who is able to sing along. Look for students who

- Know the song and handle *LMNOP* in punctuated fashion
- Need the support of the group but can keep up
- Need more practice with the song

Assess students individually to see who can point accurately as they sing or recite the letters. Prepare an alphabet strip like the one on page 95. Ask students to touch and name each letter. Record results on the Emergent Assessment Summary Sheet on page 14.

Alphabet Recognition Uppercase

To assess students' uppercase alphabet recognition, pull students aside individually. Using a copy of page 15, say to the student, "Put your finger on each letter and say the name of the letter. Skip the letter if you do not know its name." As each child points to and names the letters, record responses on the Emergent Assessment Summary Sheet. Indicate substitutions by writing in what the student says. If the child identifies *O* as "zero" or *I* as "one," ask what letter it could be. You can time students if you wish.

Note the ease with which students are able to name the letters. Do they respond quickly and confidently, or do they hesitate and perhaps recite the alphabet to help them recall the name of the letter? Students who score at least 16 are ready to be assessed on the lowercase recognition task.

Benchmarks

At the beginning of kindergarten, most students know the names of between 10 and 18 letters. At the end of kindergarten, students on average know all of their uppercase letters. Based on the PALS benchmarks, students who know more than nine letters often know many letter sounds and can benefit from further study of beginning consonant sounds through picture sorts.

Alphabet Recognition Lowercase

Using page 16 and the same procedure as for the uppercase letters, assess students' lowercase alphabet recognition and record results on the Emergent Assessment Summary Sheet. You can time students if you want. As before, say, "Put your finger on each letter and say the name of the letter. Skip the letter if you do not know its name." If the child identifies *l* as "one," ask the student what letter it could be. Write down what the student says if they make a substitution such as *b* for *d*. Expect that reversals will be common with young children learning the lowercase letters.

Benchmarks

According to PALS benchmarks, at the end of kindergarten, students on average know the names of 24 of the 26 lowercase letters.

Alphabet Production

If students seem to know most letters you can ask them to write the alphabet without looking at a model to assess how well they can produce the letter forms. Note if they write capitals or lowercase or both.

PHONOLOGICAL ASSESSMENTS

Rhyme Identification

Make a copy of the assessment on page 17 for each student. Fold it in half so that only one side shows at a time. You can conduct this individually or in small groups. Enter scores on the Emergent Assessment Summary Sheet.

Instructions

1. Tell the student that you want him or her to find some rhyming words. First, demonstrate the procedure by modeling with the first item. "We are going to find pictures that rhyme. Let's do one together. Put your finger on the picture of the duck. Next to the duck is a ball and a truck. What are the two things that rhyme? Listen: *duck, ball, truck.* Which ones rhyme or sound the same at the end? *Duck* and *truck* rhyme. Circle the two pictures that rhyme." Help students complete the sample item.
2. "Now you will mark the others on your own. Look at the bear, the keys, and the cheese. Circle the two things that rhyme. Listen: *bear, keys, cheese.* Which two rhyme?" Name the pictures each time for students to be sure they use the correct labels and guide them in the completion of this assessment.

The picture words used in the Rhyme Identification assessment are as follows.

*	<u>duck</u>	ball	<u>truck</u>
1.	bear	<u>keys</u>	<u>cheese</u>
2.	<u>bed</u>	<u>bread</u>	sock
3.	<u>mop</u>	jar	<u>shop</u>
4.	box	<u>bell</u>	<u>shell</u>

5.	<u>bug</u>	<u>rug</u>	cat
6.	<u>snake</u>	<u>cake</u>	fish
7.	feet	<u>pan</u>	<u>man</u>
8.	<u>clock</u>	<u>rock</u>	fan
9.	<u>star</u>	glass	<u>car</u>

Beginning Sounds: Alliteration

Make a copy of the assessment on page 18 for each student. You can conduct this individually or in small groups. Do not do it immediately after the rhyme assessment because students will find it confusing to shift their attention to the beginning of words after listening to the ends. Enter scores on the Emergent Assessment Summary Sheet.

Instructions

1. Begin by modeling the first item. "We are going to find pictures that begin with the same sound. Let's do one together. Put your finger on the sun. Say the word *sun*. Now look at the pictures beside the sun. Say them with me: *book, soap, jet*. Which one begins with the same sound as *sun*? *Sun* and *soap* begin with the same sound. They begin with /s/." (Say the sound, not the letter.) "Circle the picture that sounds like the first picture." Help students complete the sample item.

2. Name the rest of the pictures for students to be sure they use the correct labels and guide them in the completion of this assessment. Say the words naturally and do not overly elongate the initial sound.

The picture words used in the Beginning Sound Identification assessment are as follows. Correct responses are underlined:

*	sun	book	<u>soap</u>	jet
1.	nose	fan	kite	<u>nine</u>
2.	rabbit	<u>rug</u>	dog	leaf
3	lamp	cat	toes	<u>log</u>
4.	watch	<u>web</u>	zero	van
5.	belt	kitten	yo-yo	<u>bird</u>
6.	pie	<u>pig</u>	ball	gum
7.	zebra	key	<u>zipper</u>	hand
8.	dog	jet	leaf	<u>desk</u>

Benchmarks

By the end of kindergarten students should complete seven out of eight correctly.

LETTER–SOUND ASSESSMENTS

Assessment of Beginning Consonant Sounds and Letters

In this assessment (pages 19 and 20) students are given a letter and told to circle the picture that begins with that letter. If students score at least four on the first page, continue to the second page. Do this assessment with students who know at least half of their alphabet letters. Enter the score on the Emergent Assessment Summary Sheet.

Instructions

1. "We are going to find pictures that begin with certain letters. Let's do one together. Put your finger on the letter *m*. Circle the picture that starts with the sound the *m* makes: *kite, man, soap*. Which begins with *m*? (Say the letter.) "Yes, *man* begins with *m*, so circle it." Help students complete the sample item.

2. Name the pictures for students to be sure they use the correct labels and guide them in the completion of this assessment.

The picture words used in the Beginning Consonant Sounds assessment are as follows. Correct responses are underlined:

Beginning Consonant Sounds (1)

*	Mm	kite	<u>man</u>	soap
1.	Pp	<u>pig</u>	moon	gum
2.	Ss	block	cap	<u>sink</u>
3.	Nn	bowl	<u>nest</u>	dog
4.	Ff	sock	<u>foot</u>	cat
5.	Gg	<u>game</u>	seal	rabbit
6.	Kk	rug	<u>king</u>	mouse
7.	Ll	bun	car	<u>leaf</u>
8.	Ww	<u>watch</u>	zoo	bird

Beginning Consonant Sounds (2)

9.	Tt	map	<u>tack</u>	rope
10.	Cc	zipper	pan	<u>cat</u>
11.	Yy	bat	<u>yo-yo</u>	fork
12.	Bb	<u>bird</u>	sheep	mop
13.	Dd	sled	<u>door</u>	horse
14.	Jj	<u>jump</u>	bag	comb
15.	Rr	lamp	fish	<u>rock</u>
16.	Hh	cake	<u>hill</u>	needle

Benchmarks

By the end of kindergarten students should be able to identify the correct response in 6 of 8 (for assessment 1) or 14 of 16 (for both).

Observing Students' Writing

Students' independent writing offers information that can be recorded on the Emergent Class Record form on page 21. By capturing the change from scribbling to letterlike forms to random letters that characterize developmental changes in the early emergent stage, it can be used in preschool and kindergarten to create a class profile based on your observation of student writing or in place of the feature guide and class composites for the Primary Spelling Inventory found in *Words Their Way*. The information you collect from students' efforts to write daily in journals or labeling pictures should be used to corroborate what you find when you administer a spelling inventory. If students are not using any letter–sound correspondences in their writing, even when prompted to "Write the sounds you hear," you may decide not to administer the spelling assessment described next until later in the year.

Kindergarten Spelling Inventory (KSI)

Using a developmental assessment such as one of the spelling inventories described in *Words Their Way* is a useful way to find out if your students are able to identify and write the sounds they hear in words. We have included the Kindergarten Spelling Inventory (KSI) in this text as a resource to better understand what alphabetic clues your students may be using or not using in their writing. A form is provided on page 22 to duplicate for each student. Note that the bottom half of the form should be folded up so that it is out of sight while students are writing the words. The KSI gives you information about students' abilities to segment phonemes (i.e., break words into sounds) and choose phonetically acceptable letters to represent the beginning, middle, or ending sounds of simple short vowel words. The KSI is adapted from the PALS-K Assessment (Invernizzi, Juel, Swank, & Meier, 2007).

- To prepare students for this assessment you should conduct several lessons such as the one described in Chapter 2 of *Words Their Way* in which students are introduced to the idea of "spelling the best they can."
- You will be asking students to spell only five words. Students are not to study these words because doing so invalidates the goal of finding out what they truly know about phonics and spelling. Do *not* pre-teach these words and do *not* have them displayed during testing.
- Most teachers find it easiest to administer this assessment in small groups. Seat students so that they cannot see the papers of their classmates. Manila folders sat on end can provide a screen.
- Model *mat* as a practice item, helping students to focus on the letter sounds by stretching out or repeating the sounds made by the letters. Sounds are indicated in the directions between slash marks / /. Do not demonstrate the sounding-out process beyond the *mat* example. You may prompt students by saying, "What else do you hear? Do you hear any other sounds in the word _____?"
- Point out the picture of the word as you dictate it to give students visual support for what you are saying.
- Observe the students' writing. If you are not sure about the intended letter due to poor letter formation, ask the student what letter he or she has written or ask the student to point to the letter he or she meant to write on the alphabet strip. To help with scoring, write the intended letters above the student's attempt.

Instructions

1. Tell the students that you want them to spell some words. First, demonstrate the procedure by thinking aloud, using a blackboard or chart paper. Say, "We're going to spell some words. I'll go first. The word I want to spell is *mat*. I am going to begin by saying the word slowly. *MMM-AAA-TTT*. Now I'm going to think about each sound I hear. Listen. *MMM*. I hear an /m/ sound so I will write down the letter *m*. *MMM-AAA*. After the /m/, I hear an /ah/ sound so I will write down the letter *a*. *MMM-AAA-TTT*. At the end of the word, I hear a /t/ sound, so I will write down the letter *t*."

2. Say, "Now I want you to spell some words. Put down a letter for each sound you hear. You can use the alphabet strip at the top of your sheet if you forget how to make a letter. Ready?" Ask the students to spell the following words in this order:

1. nap
2. kid
3. log
4. jet
5. gum

A picture of each word is next to the line where it should be written. These pictures are additional support for identifying the word you are saying. The picture is not a substitute for your oral dictation.

Scoring

Please note that spelling is scored based on phonetically acceptable letter–sound matches because we are interested in whether students are able to segment the individual phonemes and choose a logical letter to represent each one. Therefore, you may see more than one possible phonetic representation for each sound. For example, *b* and *p* are often confused because they are articulated the same way and differ only because *b* is voiced and *p* is unvoiced. Read more about these logical substitutions in *Words Their Way*.

- Compare students' spelling to the boxes on the scoring grid at the bottom of the page.
- Read the grid for each word vertically, column by column, left to right, and put a check in boxes that match the student's response. Each check is worth one point. Only one check per column is possible for each word.
- Static reversals, where the student writes a mirror image of a single letter (e.g., Я for R), and self-corrections are *not* counted as errors.
- Leave each box blank if there are no matches and proceed to the next column.
- Count the number of boxes checked in each column and record on the bottom line labeled "Spelling Feature Analysis."
- Add all points and record this total in the column marked "Total Phonetically Acceptable."

Benchmarks

A score of 12 out of 15 is the benchmark for the end of kindergarten.

CONCEPT OF WORD ASSESSMENTS

Students' ability to accurately track or point to the words of something they have memorized is easily assessed in daily classroom activities when you ask students to read for you. Below are some guidelines about how to do this more formally. (A scoring rubric adapted from PALS-K is provided for *Humpty Dumpty*, but a blank form is also provided on page 26 so you can do this with any short text that students have memorized. See Chapter 5 of *Words Their Way* for a complete discussion of concept of word.)

Instructions

1. Teach a rhyme such as *Humpty Dumpty* as a whole-class activity. Use the picture cards on page 23 to teach it orally first by enlarging them and holding up a picture for each line. Practice until children have memorized it.

2. Make a printed copy of the rhyme (page 23) or write it on a chart or sentence strips and present it so that all can see. Explain, "This time as I say the rhyme I am going to

point to the words." Model saying the rhyme slowly enough to point to each word. Then ask the students to say it along with you as you point again.

3. Assess concept of word with one child at a time. Make a copy of the poem for the student to read and a copy of the word list (page 24). Make a copy of the teacher recording sheet (page 25) for each student. If you are not sure whether students have memorized the poem have them recite it using the pictures as prompts before they are asked to read it.

4. Have each student read the poem. Say, "Read *Humpty Dumpty* to me and point to the words as you read." Note whether the student has accurately tracked each line, and use the rubric to score each child's efforts from 0 to 6 for each line. Score each line of the rhyme and then compute an average. Transfer this to the Emergent Assessment Summary Sheet.

0   No left to right directionality established. May go right to left or change directions.
1   Points left to right but pointing seems vague or random with no consistent units.
2   Points to a letter for each syllable or rhythmic beat.
3   Points to words for each rhythmic beat or syllable, getting off track.
4   Points accurately to words but gets off track on two-syllable words.
5   Points accurately, getting off track on two-syllable words, but self-corrects.
6   Points accurately.

Word Recognition in Context

Point to the selected words on the student's copy of *Humpty Dumpty* (they are underlined on the teacher recording sheet) and say, "Can you tell me this word?" Give one point for each word that is correctly identified. Note strategies used by the student. Did he reread to figure out the word or did he name it immediately? Ask how he knew a word. He may say, "I knew it was *horses* because it started with *h*."

Word Recognition in Isolation

If a student's concept of word score is 4 or better you can also assess the student's recall of words in isolation. Use the list of words from page 24. Point to each word in turn, and ask the student to say the words she can read in the list. Note correct responses on the right-hand side of the teacher recording sheet and then transfer scores to the Emergent Assessment Summary Sheet.

Benchmarks

At the beginning of kindergarten most children in the early emergent stage will score between 1 and 3 on concept of word and will identify few, if any, words even in context. By the end of kindergarten most students should have a *rudimentary* concept of word and score 4 to 5 (pointing to words but occasionally getting off track). They will be slow and hesitant about identifying words you point to but will know some of them. Students who consistently score 5 to 6 have a *full* concept of word and are probably in the letter name–alphabetic stage of spelling. They should be able to identify nearly all words quickly in context (6 of 7) and will identify most of the words in the list (7 of 10).

REFERENCE

Invernizzi, M., Juel, C., Swank, L., & Meier, J. (2007). *Phonological Awareness Literacy Screening-Kindergarten (PALS-K)*. Charlottesville: University of Virginia Printing.

Emergent Assessment Summary Sheet

Name _____ Date _____ Teacher _____

Alphabet Tracking Observations

Alphabet Recognition: Capitals

M P S O X N A F G K L T U C Y

B I V D J E Q R Z H W   Number Correct ___

Alphabet Recognition: Lowercase

m p s o x n a f g k l t u c y

b i v d j e q r z h w   Number Correct ___

Rhyme Identification   ___/9

Beginning Sounds: Alliteration   ___/8

Beginning Letter–Sounds Identification   ___/8   ___/8   Total ____/16

Kindergarten Spelling Inventory	Number of Beginning Phonemes	Number of Middle Phonemes	Number of Ending Phonemes	Total Phonetically Acceptable
	/5	/5	/5	/15

Concept of Word:

Pointing Score Average: _____

Word Identification in Context: _____ of _____

Word List Identification: _____ of _____

Observations:

Alphabet Recognition: Uppercase

M P S O X

N A F G K

L T U C Y

B I V D J

E Q R Z H

W

m p s o x

n a f g k

l t u c y

b i v d j

e q r z h

w

Assessment for Rhyme

Instructions: Circle the two pictures that rhyme.

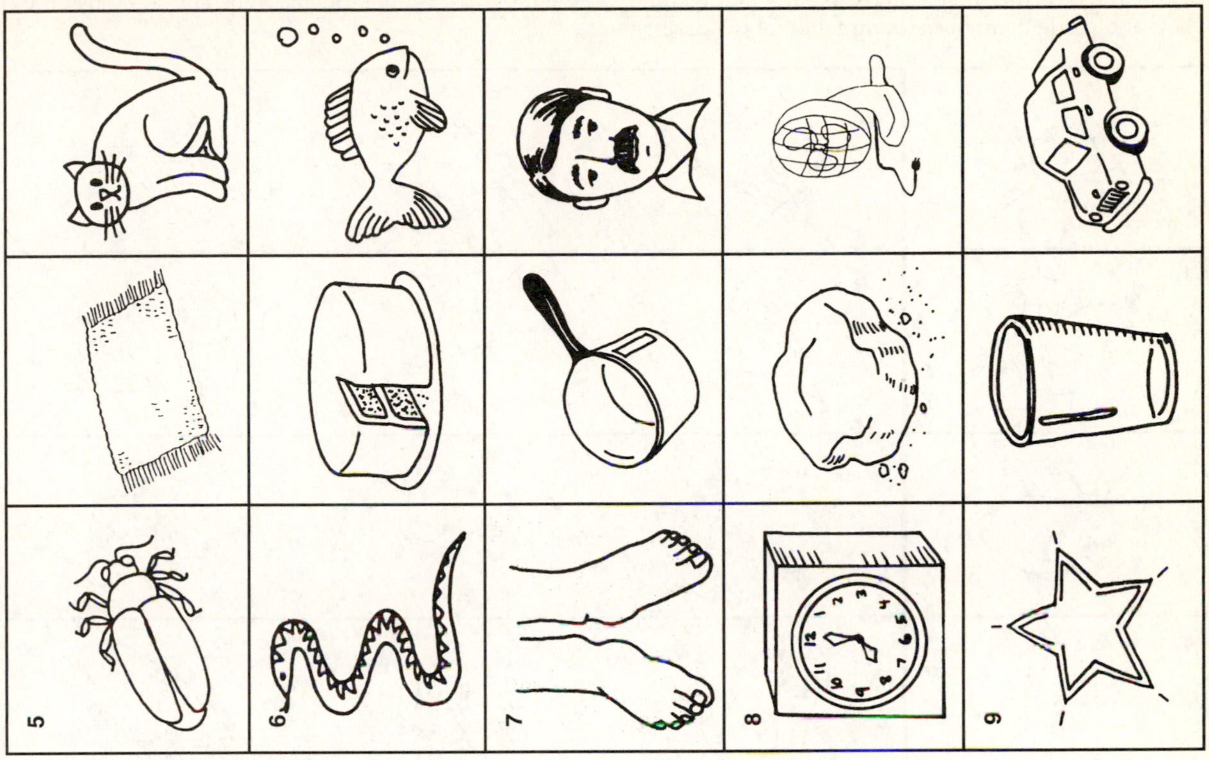

5

6

7

8

9

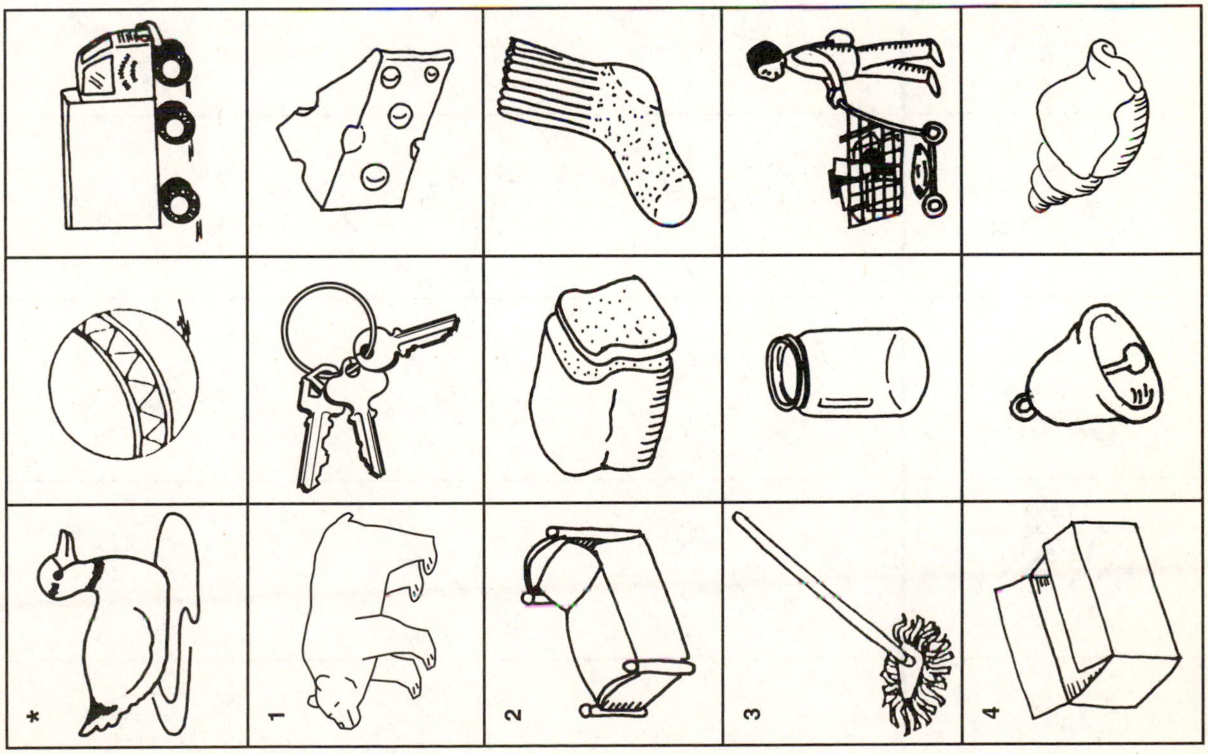

Date

Name

*

1

2

3

4

17

Beginning Sounds

Instructions: "Put your finger on the sun. Say the word *sun*. What picture sounds like *sun* at the beginning: *book, soap, jet*. Circle the picture that sounds like the first picture." Name the pictures for students to be sure they use the right labels and guide them in the completion of this assessment.

Beginning Consonant Sounds and Letters

Name _____ Date _____ # Correct _____

* **Mm**				
1 **Pp**				
2 **Ss**				
3 **Nn**				
4 **Ff**				
5 **Gg**				
6 **Kk**				
7 **Ll**				
8 **Ww**				

Beginning Consonant Sounds and Letters (continued)

Name _____ Date _____ # Correct _____

9	**Tt**			
10	**Cc**			
11	**Yy**			
12	**Bb**			
13	**Dd**			
14	**Jj**			
15	**Rr**			
16	**Hh**			

Emergent Class Record

Class Record to Assess Emergent and Letter Name – Alphabetic Stage Spelling, Pre-Kindergarten – Kindergarten

Directions: Check boxes or date entries over several observations. A check minus (✓–) indicates features used occasionally. A check plus (✓+) indicates consistent use.

Teacher _____ Class _____ Grade _____ Date(s) _____

SPELLING STAGES→	EMERGENT STAGE						LETTER NAME—ALPHABETIC STAGE				
	EARLY		MIDDLE		LATE		EARLY		MIDDLE		LATE
↓ Name of Student / Spelling Features →	Random Marks	Linear Scribbles	Letterlike Writing	Random Letters	Beginning Consonants	Final Consonants	Logical Vowel Substitutions*	Consonant Digraphs	Consonant Blends	Correct Short Vowels

*Logical vowel substitutions show how a student would use a letter name strategy to spell long vowels (as in HOP for *hope*) or short vowels (PAT for *pet* or DEG for *dig*)

Student Spelling Inventory

Name_____   Date _____

A B C D E F G H I J K L M N O P Q R S T U V W X Y Z
a b c d e f g h i j k l m n o p q r s t u v w x y z

1. _____

2. _____

3. _____

4. _____

5. _____

Adapted from PALS Quick Checks, University of Virginia

Fold here -

Scoring Grid

	Beginning	Middle	Ending	
1. nap	n	a	p	
		e	b	_____ # phonetically acceptable
2. kid	k	i	d	
	c or g	e	t	_____ # phonetically acceptable
3. log	l	o	g	
		i	k	_____ # phonetically acceptable
4. jet	j	e	t	
	g	a	d	_____ # phonetically acceptable
5. gum	g	u	m	
	k or c	o		_____ # phonetically acceptable

Spelling Feature Analysis	Number of Beginning Phonemes	Number of Middle Phonemes	Number of Ending Phonemes	Total Phonetically Acceptable
				/15

Name_____   Date/Story Number_____

Humpty Dumpty

Humpty Dumpty sat on a wall.

Humpty Dumpty had a great fall.

All the king's horses

And all the king's men

Couldn't put Humpty together again!

on

Humpty

put

horses

sat

men

king's

wall

had

fall

Concept of Word in Print with *Humpty Dumpty*

Name _____ Date _____ Teacher _____

	Pointing	Word ID	Word List
<u>Humpty</u> Dumpty sat on a <u>wall</u>		(2)	on
Humpty Dumpty had a <u>great</u> fall		(1)	Humpty
All <u>the</u> king's <u>horses</u>		(2)	put
And <u>all</u> the king's men		(1)	horses
Couldn't <u>put</u> Humpty together again		(1)	sat
Score:	Avg	/7	men
			king's
			wall
Pointing Benchmark: 6			had
Word ID Benchmark: 6/7			fall
COW Word List Benchmark: 7/10			**/10**

Scoring for Pointing

0   No left to right directionality established; may go right to left or change directions

1   Points left to right but pointing seems vague or random with no consistent units

2   Points to a letter for each syllable or rhythmic beat

3   Points to words for each rhythmic beat or syllable getting off track

4   Points accurately to words but gets off track on two-syllable words

5   Points accurately until getting off track on two-syllable words, but self-corrects

6   Points accurately

Score each line and then compute an average to record.

Observations: How readily do students identify words in context when you point to them in the rhyme? What strategies do they use when they do not know the word immediately? In the word list identification task do substitutions resemble the word, as in *house* for *horse* or *pig* for *put*?

Concept of Word Assessment

Name _____ Date _____ Teacher _____

	Pointing	Word ID	Word List
Score:	**Avg**		
Pointing Benchmark: 6			
Word ID Benchmark: 6/7			
COW Word List Benchmark: 7/10			**Total**

Scoring for Pointing

0 No left to right directionality established; may go right to left or change directions

1 Points left to right but pointing seems vague or random with no consistent units

2 Points to a letter for each syllable or rhythmic beat

3 Points to words for each rhythmic beat or syllable getting off track

4 Points accurately to words but gets off track on two-syllable words

5 Points accurately until getting off track on two-syllable words, but self-corrects

6 Points accurately

Score each line and then compute an average to record.

Observations: How readily do students identify words in context when you point to them in the rhyme? What strategies do they use when they do not know the word immediately? In the word list identification task do substitutions resemble the word, as in *house* for *horse* or *pig* for *put*?

Chapter 2   Concept Sorts

NOTES FOR THE TEACHER

Background

In this chapter we present five literacy units that center around a concept sort but also include other parts of the literacy diet: Read To, Read With, Write With, Talk With, and so on. A concept sort is an activity in which pictures, objects, or words are grouped by shared attributes. In Chapter 4 of *Words Their Way* we offer a rationale for the use of concept sorts for vocabulary growth and concept development. The introductory sorts in this section teach the process of sorting. Students acquire new vocabulary as they learn to categorize their pictures, manipulate their sort cards, name the pictures aloud, and talk about the sorts. Through these sorts you will guide students in thinking conceptually as they compare and contrast ideas and objects. Later, the foundation in vocabulary and thinking skills that has been developed through concept sorts will help you and your students be successful at working with sorts involving phonological awareness and phonics skills.

Concept sorts take advantage of the way we think in hierarchies. They are multifaceted and consist of a number of levels, parts, and subsorts, like a large tree with many branches. These concept sorts can be branched two or three ways. For example, in the first sort, the goal is to teach the rudiments of sorting, and we start with the most basic contrast: those that fit and those that do not (*fruit/not a fruit*). In the second fruit sort, students sort apples, bananas, and oranges into three columns. In open sorts, students find additional categories for sorting.

Targeted Learners

Concept sorts are an excellent way to introduce students to sorting. Everyone can participate without forming separate ability groups. Even the youngest children can take part in these concept sorts, and there are additional literacy activities for each unit that will benefit all emergent learners. However, concept sorts are not just for early emergent learners. They can be used up through the grades in many content areas.

A wonderful feature of concept sorts is that English learners of all ages can participate even without knowing the English terms, because they can use their own language to identify the pictures. English learners can describe their sorting in their own language, and you have the opportunity to connect the English vocabulary for them right in that instructional moment in very visual ways. Older students learning English particularly enjoy the more complicated extended branching of concept sorts. For example, in the living and nonliving sort, students may be assigned to draw or find pictures of the next level of the sort; for example, one student could be in charge of finding birds and learning how to sort, classify, and categorize them.

Teaching Tips

The best way to get children started in sorting is to use real physical objects. Many teachers have collections of blocks, keys, buttons, plastic animals, nuts and bolts, and so on, that can be sorted by various attributes. In the activity section of Chapter 4 in *Words Their Way* we suggest a number of concrete sorts and describe how to make and use a pasta sort. Possible concrete sorts and children's literature are also suggested in the sorts that follow here. If the books we suggest are out of print you can probably still find some of them by searching the Internet.

There are four other premade concept sorts on the *Words Their Way* CD-ROM: *work and play, clothes and body parts, transportation,* and *creatures.* There are also more ideas for children's books and follow-up concept sorts in Chapter 4 of *Words Their Way.*

STANDARD ROUTINES TO USE WITH CONCEPT SORTS

1. *Read To and Talk With.* The books you read aloud to children can often be the beginning point of a concept sort that will include opportunities to practice new vocabulary. You will see examples in this chapter. But even without the sorts, books expose children to concepts and new vocabulary. Take the time to introduce new words and explain their meanings in terms your students can understand. Encourage your students to use new words and revisit those words in other contexts. Make read-alouds interactive. Engage students in talk by asking open-ended questions and encouraging observations and comments.

2. *Label Categories.* Once categories of pictures have been established, create headers with the students' help and demonstrate how to write the headers by saying the words slowly, identifying sounds within the words, and selecting letters to represent the sounds. Students can be encouraged to use invented spelling to label categories also.

3. *Independent Sorting.* After sorting as a group activity, provide ways for students to sort again to reinforce the concepts and vocabulary. You can leave the sort in a pocket chart or center and encourage children to work together and talk about the sort. You can also make a copy of the blackline master for each student, enlarging it to reduce paper waste and increase the size of the pictures. Students can use a distinct color of crayon to quickly scribble on the back side of their paper before cutting it apart. This helps when cards get mixed up among students sitting near each other. After cutting out the pictures and working with them in open sorts (see below), the pieces can be stored in an envelope or plastic bag to use in activities on subsequent days.

4. *Conduct an Open Sort.* After a sort has been introduced and practiced, ask students to divide pictures into different groups in their own way. As they begin to sort, ask students to talk about their sort. As long as they have an organizing principle, let them continue sorting. Remember, this is an open sort, so students' categories do not need to be what you would select. When they are finished, see if the students can share how they sorted with you and the group. Students who are just beginning to learn to sort sometimes have difficulty dividing pictures by features. They may start with one idea and then switch to another. If this happens, step in to guide a little more. Ask students questions about how they are manipulating the pictures, and see if your questions help the students see characteristics in the items that could be used to group them. For example, you may ask, "Are some of these big or small?" or "Which ones look the same?"

5. *Draw and Label and Cut and Paste Activities.* A follow-up activity to concept sorts is to ask students to draw more things that go into a category or to look for pictures that they can cut out of magazines and catalogs. Model this first with the whole group and then have children draw or hunt for pictures under your supervision. Create one large chart after labeling the categories. Once children understand how to complete these activities they can do them with a partner or independently. Create a sorting surface by folding a large sheet of paper into two or four categories. Students then draw or paste pictures in the correct spaces. They should be encouraged to label the categories using invented spelling. Find time for children to talk with each other about their pictures.

6. *Extend Through Other Literacy Activities.* Add Read With and more Write With activities as well as alphabet activities, rhyme sorts, and beginning sound sorts when appropriate. In the lessons that follow you will see examples of these and how the complete literacy diet is covered.

UNIT 1: FRUIT

This first unit includes the most basic of sorts and is easy to introduce. There are two sorts here: *Fruit/Not Fruit* and *Apples, Bananas, and Oranges.* Integrated into this unit are several literacy activities. Take your time and model carefully if this is your students' first sort.

Read With: *My Fruit*

The reading selections presented in this supplement are introduced in Read With activities when students begin to memorize at least one or two lines. These simple rhymes and jingles can be enlarged through overheads, made into handouts, written on chart paper, and posted around the room so that students refer to them often in word and letter hunts. We urge you to collect these familiar selections in personal readers as described in Chapter 6. Learning to point accurately is a priority throughout the emergent stage, so children should have copies of text at their fingertips.

Read the selection on page 42 titled *My Fruit* to your students. On a second reading, have students join in peeling, cutting, and washing motions while echoing the words. On subsequent readings model how you point to the words. Students should reread as many lines as possible, but focus on just one to three lines if they flounder on more. Students may not know what it means to *peel* a piece of fruit or to *slice* a banana. Bring in real fruit to wash, peel, and cut up. Take time to introduce the vocabulary in this sort.

My Fruit
I peel, peel, peel my banana.
I cut, cut, cut my banana.
And I put the banana in a bowl.
I wash, wash, wash my apple.
I cut, cut, cut my apple.
And I put the apple in a bowl.
I peel, peel, peel my orange.
I cut, cut, cut my orange.
And I put the orange in a bowl.

Concept Sort 1: Fruit/Not Fruit

Make a copy of the pictures for Fruit/Not Fruit on page 43 and cut them apart for sorting (or start with a sort of plastic fruit and nonfood objects such as blocks, toys, or other

Literature Connection

Share these and other books that feature fruit before or after introducing the sort.

Ehlert, L. (1989). *Eating the alphabet.* New York: Trumpet Club.

Freymann, S., & Elffers, J. (1999). *How are you peeling?* New York: Scholastic.

Lember, B. H. (1994). *A book of fruit.* New York: Ticknor & Fields.

Schuette, S. L. (2003). *An alphabet salad: Fruits and vegetables from A to Z.* Mankato, MN: Capstone Press.

small objects from the classroom). Explain to your students, "Here are some pictures to sort. Let's name them together." Read through the pictures and explain that some of the pictures are fruits and others are not fruits. Introduce the *apple* and the *hat* as key pictures: "Here is a picture of an apple. An apple is a fruit and I am going to put it here at the top." Hold up the picture of the hat. "What is this? A hat, yes. A hat is not a fruit! What do you do with fruit? You EAT it. Would you eat a hat?" (Children will enjoy the silliness of this idea.) "I am going to put the picture of the hat over here" (to the right of the apple). "Now, I am going to give you a picture to sort. Show us where your picture goes. If it is a picture of a fruit, put it underneath the picture of the apple. If it is not a fruit, put your picture underneath the hat."

Sort, Check, and Reflect

Explain to students how to check their sort: "When we are all done, we name the pictures in each column and check our work. Watch me—apple, orange, banana, apples, bananas, oranges. If we find one that does not belong we make a change." Go through the non-fruit pictures to check and reflect on why you are sorting the way you are. Create a label for each sort by writing "Fruit "and "Not Fruit" on a card eliciting student help and modeling how to stretch out the sounds and find letters. Sort one more time in the group.

Use prepared sorts, or have students work in pairs to cut up one sort to work together. Remind students that *apple* and *hat* are the key pictures for sorting and should be put at the top of the columns. Help students to reflect on why they sorted the way they did: "These are fruits that I can eat and these are things that I would not eat." Pictures are stored in individual baggies after sorting.

Fruit	Not Fruit
apple	**hat**
banana	comb
orange	ring
2 bananas	bat
2 apples	rain
2 oranges	map
cut apple	rake
cut banana	
cut orange	

Sort a Different Way

The next day ask students to sort again the same way they did yesterday; then explain that the pictures can be sorted another way. Pull out pictures of apples, bananas, and oranges to use as key pictures or headers and have students do the same thing. Tell them to sort the pictures under these new headers. A third sort can be done using the following key pictures: 1 banana, 2 bananas, and cut banana. Set up the headers and see if students can sort appropriately. Each of the sorts is shown below. Expect that changing the key pictures for sorting will pose problems for some students and be ready to model explicitly as needed.

Demonstrate the sort using the key pictures from the fruit sort, naming the pictures with the students.

Apples	Bananas	Oranges	Ones	Twos	Cuts
apple	banana	orange	banana	2 bananas	cut banana
2 apples	2 bananas	2 oranges	apple	2 apples	cut apple
cut apple	cut banana	cut orange	orange	2 oranges	cut orange

Conduct sorts in small groups until students can complete these on their own. Help students to reflect on why they sorted the way they did: "I sorted the fruit in this way: The fruits here beginning with the apple have one piece of fruit, the fruits in this column have two pieces of fruit, and the cut pieces are in this group."

Read With

Reread *My Fruit*. Students fingerpoint read *My Fruit* using their own copies of the text. Model as needed for students who require assistance explaining how to track: "Put your finger on the title, *My Fruit*. Put your finger on the first line, *I peel, peel, peel my banana*." Track the next line of text. Students fingerpoint read the same line of text on their individual copies. Recite and reread as often as possible: in the morning, in reading groups, independently, and to others at home.

Talk With and Write With:
Collect a One-Sentence Dictation

Familiar reading materials are created when you take dictations from students. Fruits provide powerful experiences for student enjoyment and verbal interaction so bring in a few pieces of fruit to taste for a language experience. Listen for and use related vocabulary: *fruit, peel, seeds, rind, skin, sweet, sour, ripe*.

To prompt a dictation you might say, "What is your favorite fruit?" As you take a dictation, write so that the child can see what you are doing. Say each word slowly as you write and talk about what you are doing: "I will start with a capital letter here and end with a period." As children develop letter–sound knowledge, ask them to help you decide what letters to use: "What letter will I need to write the the first sound in the word *banana*?" After writing the sentence, read it back as you point to the words and ask the child if you got it right: "This says, *Jason likes bananas*." Students can draw pictures to accompany their dictations. These dictations can be placed in their personal readers (page 168) to reread regularly and use as a source for word hunts.

Letter and Word Hunts

Use the reading selection *My Fruit* and ask students to hunt for letters and words. For example, in a letter hunt you might ask, "Find the letter *b*. Find a word that starts with *b*. Can you find another one?" Observe to find out what letters students know and how quickly they find them. Children who know most of their letters can be challenged to look for words: "Let's find some words: Put your finger on the word *I*. Find the word *banana* at the end of this line."

Extend

Extend with a picture hunt and cutting and pasting. Do this first as a large-group activity. Provide magazines that are likely to have pictures of fruit and ask students to cut out pictures of fruit and not fruit. Students can also be asked to bring pictures from home. With their help label a chart with the same headers you used before—"Fruit" and "Not Fruit." After children have found several pictures come together as a group and sort them under the headers. There may be some discussion of whether a carrot or potato is a fruit or not. Once the pictures have been sorted they should be glued in place.

Include other fruit in a sort. A grape is another fruit you can use to introduce new vocabulary: "Grapes come in *bunches* and have *stems*." A song about fruit that children will enjoy is *Apples and Bananas* by Raffi. This song plays with sounds as the vowels in the words are changed ("*Epples and beneenees*"). Language play like this can enhance children's phonological awareness.

UNIT 2: SHAPES: CIRCLES, TRIANGLES, AND SQUARES

Shapes and the language of shapes are basic to early childhood curriculum, and shapes lend themselves readily to sorting. We suggest starting with circles, triangles, and squares.

Sort 2A: Shapes

Make a copy of the pictures of circles, triangles, and squares for sorting on page 44 (or collect real objects that can be sorted on the basis of their shapes—books, dishes, puzzle pieces, blocks, and so on). Name the objects and pictures and listen for students who know the names of the shapes. Then pull out the pictures of the circle, triangle, and square that are underlined and say, "Here are three shapes to sort: circles, triangles, and squares. Let's look for other things that have these shapes." The final sort will look like this:

Circle	Triangle	Square
cookie	traffic sign	puzzle
1 circle inside another	2 triangles	block
sun	1 triangle inside another	2 squares
2 circles	triangle bell	picture frame
		1 square within another

Literature Connection

Carle, E. (1974). *My very first book of shapes.* New York: HarperCollins.

Baker, A. (1999). *Brown Rabbit's shape book.* New York: Kingfisher.

Dotich, R. (1999). *What is round? and What is a triangle?* New York: HarperFestival.

Hoban, T. (1996). *Shapes, shapes, shapes.* New York: HarperTrophy.

Hoban, T. (1998). *So many circles, so many squares.* New York: Greenwillow.

Kaczman, J. (2001). *When a line bends . . . a shape begins.* Boston: Houghton Mifflin.

Create headers by writing the words for the shapes and then make a copy for students to sort on their own. Encourage students to look for objects in the room that have the same shapes. Help them to differentiate squares and rectangles.

Sort 2B: Other Attributes of the Shapes

The second shape sort, on page 45, is more complex and can be pursued once there is success with the first. Students sort these shapes by their outline forms—dashes, stripes, shaded, and outlined shapes—and should be encouraged to describe similarities and differences. The concepts and vocabulary (stripes, dashes) may be new to many students.

Dashed Circle	**Dashed Triangle**	**Dashed Square**
striped circle	striped triangle	striped square
shaded circle	shaded triangle	shaded square
several shaded circles	several shaded triangles	several shaded squares
outlined circle	outlined triangle	outlined square

Sort, Check, and Reflect

Give each student a collection of pictures to sort in a small group sort. Continue to show students how to match the pictures they are sorting to the key pictures at the top. To check, begin with the key pictures and read down the columns. Explain: "Let's name each column to check our sort."

Continue to model the language of reflection: "How did we sort these pictures? These are all circles, these are triangles, and these are squares. These have four corners, these have three corners, and these have no corners."

Talk With

By explaining as you sort, you'll use vocabulary that may be new to students. Key terms include: *corners, round, points, lines, angles, striped, shaded, outlined.*

English learners may understand the English from their knowledge of other Romance languages. For example, the English and Spanish terms are similar: *circle/circulo, triangle/triángulo, square/cuadrado (plaza), rectangle/rectángulo.*

Extend

Share books about shapes such as the ones listed above. Lay out a rope in the shape of the figures. Have students walk around the shapes. Discuss what they do at the corners.

Have students draw around the shapes with crayons. As they color, engage them in discussions about their favorite colors or the colors they are using. Do they know colors, shapes, and sizes? Cut and paste magazine pictures with these shapes.

Read With: *Circles*

Prepare to read the selection on page 46 titled *Circles.* Make a transparency, create a chart, or place a paper copy in front so all can see. Also prepare a copy for each child. After reading the selection the first time, have students make shapes with large arm movements as you read it again.

Track one line of text at a time. Students can echo and fingerpoint read the same line of text on their individual copies. Model as students need assistance. "Put your finger on the title, *Circles*. Put your finger on the first line, "I make circles." If students can point to the words, watch to see when they are thrown off by a two-syllable word (e.g., *circles* or *paper*). Students can draw circles on their paper to illustrate the poem.

> **Circles**
>
> I make circles.
> I make circles in the air.
> I make circles on paper.
> I make circles on the board.

Letter and Word Hunts

Ask students to look for letters: "Find the letter *m*." Make note of the letters that students know and how quickly they find them. You can also ask students to hunt for letters that have circles: *o*, *p*, *b*, and so on.

Students who can point with some accuracy can look for words: "Let's find some words: Put your finger on the word *circles*. Let's go to the next line. Put your finger on the word *I*. Find the next word, the word that begins with the *mmm* sound. *Mmmmake*."

Write With

The poem can be expanded for oral language development. "How else can we make circles? *I make circles _____*" (with a crayon, with paint, and with blocks). You can take a one-sentence dictation that begins, "*I make circles _____.*"

UNIT 3: ANIMALS AND PLANTS

This unit includes a two-part sort. Interesting and complex questions arise when we define what an animal is. Do all animals have legs? Do all animals move? What are the differences between the land and water animals? What makes birds and insects fly?

Concept Sort 3: Animals

Make a copy of the sort for Animal/Not an Animal on page 47. Read the pictures with students. Explain: "Here is a picture of a horse. A horse is an animal. Let's look at the next picture, a tree. A tree is not an animal, so I am going to put the picture of the tree over here." After the group sort have students sort their own copies of the sort

Literature Connection

There are hundreds of books that feature animals. Here are a few.

Campbell, R. (1982). *Dear zoo.* Salem, OR: Four Winds.

Christalow, E. (1999). *Five little monkeys jumping on the bed.* Boston: Clarion.

Hoban, T. (1985). *A children's zoo.* New York: Greenwillow.

Rey, H. R. (1941). *Curious George.* Boston: Houghton Mifflin.

Walsh, M. (1996). *Do pigs have stripes?* Boston: Houghton Mifflin.

Wells, R. (1998). *Old MacDonald.* New York: Scholastic.

independently or with a partner. Reflect by talking about attributes of animals (e.g., they move, they grow, they need food and water to live). Create labels for the two categories.

Animal	Not an Animal
horse	tree
monkey	rope
rabbit	rock
turtle	wheat
dog	pine tree
whale	rose
bear	daisy
butterfly	grass
cat	cactus
bird	potted plant
worm	car
girl	
fish	

Sort Again: Animals and Plants

Push the animals to one side and ask students to look at the pictures that are left. "Do you see any pictures that go together?" With students help subdivide the non-animal column into two columns: plants and pictures that do not fit. Pictures of the rock and the rope are set aside. "Is a rope an animal? Is a rope a plant? I am going to put this picture to the side over here with other pictures that do not fit; they are not animals or plants." Create labels for the new categories. Combine all the pictures and resort into groups, putting them in three categories: animals, plants, and those that do not fit.

Sort, Check, and Reflect

The next day have students repeat the sort and review why they sorted as they did. Ask them how plants are alike. Ask students to name the pictures in each column of their own sorts to check their work.

Animal	Plant	
horse	tree	rock
monkey	cactus	car
rabbit	wheat	rope
turtle	rose	
dog	daisy	
whale	grass	
bear	pine tree	
butterfly	potted plant	
cat		
bird		
worm		
girl		
fish		

Extend

Have students search through selected pages from magazines for pictures of animals and plants, then cut and paste the pictures onto one page. These pages can be displayed around the room. If you have plastic or stuffed animals, students can sort them into categories of their choosing.

Talk With

There are many animals and plants, and there are many ways to describe the features of each animal and plant. You may find several other categories in students' discussions of these animals: how animals move (fly, swim, walk), where animals live (water, woods, farm, zoo), number of legs, indoor or outdoor plants or animals, useful to people or not, and so on. A sort for zoo animals and farm animals is described in *Words Their Way*.

Once these subcategories are established, additional examples will come to students' minds. For example, for flying animals, flies, pigeons, moths, and different types of birds may be added; and for water animals, there are different forms of fish, penguins, sea lions, dolphins, crabs, and sea stars.

Read With: *Animals*

The selection on page 48 is a poem titled *Animals* that invites movements. Prepare copies to use as you read it with the children. Ask three or four students to demonstrate movements for others to enjoy, clapping after each group performance. Students raise their voices with the excitement of jumping like monkeys. Point out the exclamation mark: "An exclamation mark shows excitement."

Animals
Birds fly in the air.
Fish swim in the water.
And monkeys jump
Everywhere!

Write With

Students enjoy dictating sentences about their favorite animals. You can ask students to include a color in their one-sentence dictations to create something like *Green crocodiles swim in the water*. Students can draw pictures to go with their dictations. Have students try to fingerpoint read their one-sentence dictations.

Sound Hunts

Choose a word from *Animals*: "Listen for words that begin with the same sound that you hear in *bird*. What is the first letter in *bird*? What is the first sound? I am going to say two words. Do they have the same sound at the beginning?" For example, "*birds–baby*, yes. *birds–fish*, no." Emphasize the sound at the beginning of each word. Other frequently occurring consonants include *m* as in *monkeys* and *f* as in *fish*. Prepare a beginning sound sort for these consonant sounds following the steps in Chapter 5.

UNIT 4: CLOTHING

Concept Sort 4: Clothes

Prepare a copy of the sort for clothes on page 49. Name the pictures with students. Get ideas from them about how to sort the pictures. Select pictures of the hat, shoes, coat,

Literature Connection

Barrett, J. (1988). *Animals should definitely not wear clothing*. New York: Aladdin Library.

London, J. (1989). *Froggy gets dressed*. New York: Viking.

Neitzel, S. (1989). *This is the jacket I wear in the snow*. New York: Greenwillow.

Peek, M. (1982). *Mary wore her red dress and Henry wore his green sneakers*. Boston: Clarion.

Taback, S. (1999). *Joseph had a little overcoat*. New York: Scholastic.

Wells, R. (1991). *Max's dragon shirt*. New York: Dial.

and gloves that are underlined. Establish columns by talking about where each item is worn on the body. "Here is a hat. Where do you wear a hat? On your head." Pass out pictures to students, and model for them how to contribute to the sort: "Where do you wear skates? We will put skates under the shoes because we wear them on our feet." The scarf might be set aside since it is worn around the neck.

Head	Feet	Body	Hands	
cap	shoes	coat	gloves	scarf
stocking cap	work boots	sweater	mittens	
man's hat	girl's shoes	shirt	work gloves	
crown	running shoes	jacket		
lady's hat	boots	swimsuit		
	slippers	shorts		
	skates			
	sandals			
	socks			

Extend

Ask students if they can think of other ways to sort the pictures of clothing. Some items come in pairs while others do not. Some items keep you warm in the winter while others would be worn in the summer or inside.

This sort easily extends to physical object sorts. Try a "guess my category" sort with categories such as: shirts with buttons and without; short-sleeved shirts and long-sleeved shirts; shorts, long pants, and skirts; or shoes with laces, shoes with velcro, slip-on shoes, and so on. Ask children to move to an area of the room without telling them the category. See if they can figure out how everyone in the group is alike. Button sorts are a favorite and tie in here too!

Read With: *Socks, Shoes, Caps, and Gloves*

The four-line selection on page 50 is easy to recite with movements and the single-syllable words will make it easy to track. Model and then have children track their own copies.

Socks, Shoes, Caps, and Gloves

I put socks over my toes.
I put shoes on my feet.
I put a cap on my head.
I put gloves on my hands.

Word Study

A number of concrete words start with beginning consonants in this selection. For example, *h* (*head* and *hands*), *s* (*socks*), *t* (*toes*), *c* (*cap*), and *f* (*feet*) could all be the starting point for a consonant sort as described in Chapter 5.

Talk With and Write With

Over and *on* and similar prepositions in this story can become sorting categories: *"I put my shorts on, I put my sweater over my head, I put my scarf around my neck."* There are many activities with the hand and body that can form the basis for Talk With and Write With activities. For example, young students like to draw around the shape of their hands with a crayon and then dictate a sentence like *"My hand is on the paper."*

UNIT 5: CLEANING

In this sort students will categorize things they use for personal cleaning and those they would use to clean the house.

Learn the Song: *This Is the Way*

The traditional song "Here We Go Round the Mulberry Bush" has been adapted slightly. Teach children to sing it while acting out motions.

> This is the way we wash our hands.
> Wash our hands, wash our hands.
> This is the way we wash our hands
> So early in the morning.

Ask the children about other things they do to clean themselves and make up other verses like "This is the way we wash our face," "This is the way we brush our teeth," and so on. Then talk about cleaning the house. What can they do to help? Make up more verses like "This is the way we sweep the floor" or "This is the way we clean the sink," and so on. In each case act out the words with motions and with objects if available.

Concept Sort 5: Cleaning

Make a copy of the pictures for cleaning on page 51 to model the concept sort for cleaning. Pick up a picture such as the mop and ask, "Would you use this to clean yourself or the house? The house, of course! Let's put it over here. How about a toothbrush? Would you use that to clean yourself or the house?" Continue to sort all the pictures under either the mop or the toothbrush. (A third category can be added if students say that

---

Literature Connection

The books below have additional verses that students will enjoy after making up their own.

Fatus, S. (2008). *Here we go round the mulberry bush* (with CD). Cambridge, MA: Barefoot Books.

Kubler, A., & Freeman, T. (2001). *Here we go round the mulberry bush*. Wiltshire, UK: Child's Play (International).

something can be used for either. For example, some may say they use a sponge to wash themselves.) The sort will look something like this:

toothbrush	mop
soap	pail
towel	vacuum
tub	broom
comb	sponge
toothpaste	spray bottle of cleaner
shampoo	brush
sink	

Check and Reflect

Ask children to come up with a label for each category. It might be "Me" and "House." Write the labels with their help. Then pass out the pictures and sort again, making sure that each item is named before it is sorted. Pick out an object like the vacuum and demonstrate how to make up a new verse to the song such as "This is the way I vacuum the rug." Then let children take turns selecting a picture and making up an appropriate verse.

Make a copy of the sort for children to cut apart and sort on their own or with a partner. Move around as they sort and ask them to name the pictures or to sing a verse to go with a picture. Later, ask children to come up with their own categories.

Read With: *This Is the Way*

The selection on page 52 can be introduced on a second day after children have sung the song again, recreating some of the verses from the day before. Create a large copy of the first verse and point to the words as you read them. Then ask the students to read along with you. Give each student a copy of the song to practice tracking. Make a copy of the song to post over the sink where children wash their hands before snack or lunch. Encourage the children to sing the song while they soap their hands to ensure that they wash them long enough to get them really clean. You might add a second verse that says "This is the way I dry my hands."

Talk With and Write With

Remind the students that they were able to make up lots of new verses to the song and select one or two to record on a chart. Pictures from the sort can be added to illustrate the different verses.

Then give students a copy of the song with blank spaces (see page 53) and discuss what they would like to write. Meet with children individually to write in the words they want to add or encourage them to write for themselves, spelling the best they can. This song can be changed to include all kinds of classroom routines such as "This is the way we pick up blocks" or "This is way we go to lunch."

Word Study

Go on a letter hunt for the letter *W* and talk about the sound at the beginning of *way, we,* and *wash.* This is a troublesome letter because it has a three-syllable name and the name does not offer a clue to the sound it represents.

UNIT 6: FOODS

Concept Sort 6: Food

Food sorts are complex because we have so many associations with food—when we eat it and how it is prepared. To assess students' knowledge of sorting, the concept of open sorts is introduced. In open sorts, students define the categories for sorting, giving a window into their thinking.

Prepare the sort on page 54. Remember to enlarge it to eliminate the border. Begin by naming the pictures with the students. Note what pictures students can recognize and name, and for English language learners, what language they use to read the pictures. Give all the students a set of pictures to cut out (or have them cut in advance) and explain: "Today, you will find your own way of sorting the pictures. Take the pictures you know, and sort them into three or four groups." Have students explain why they sorted the way they did.

For students who are unable to get started, you may suggest groups in this way: "If I put this picture with this one, can you guess why?" For example, carrots and peas could be paired. Often this is enough to get them to find a third picture. Then bring the students together and do a group sort. Create labels that describe the categories. The final sort might look like this:

Baked Items	Drinks	Vegetables	Fruit	
bread	pitcher and glass	beans	apple	eggs
taco	tea or coffee	lettuce	banana	soup
roll	soda bottle	carrots	cherries	
pizza	juice pack	tomatoes	watermelon	
pancake	milk	potatoes	pineapple	
		peas	grapes	

Assess Concept Sorting

Assess students' engagement and understanding of the principles and procedures of sorting as they do an open sort using the questions that follow. Students who sort accurately and competently are ready to sort independently for repeated practice at their seats or in centers.

Literature Connection

You can read about food using books such as those listed below.

Brown, M. (1991). *Sopa de piedras/Stone soup.* New York: Lectorum Publications.
    This story lends itself well to dramatization.

Carle, E. (1993). *Today is Monday.* New York: Scholastic.

Ehlert, L. (1989). *Eating the alphabet.* Orlando, FL: Harcourt.

Fleming, D. (1992). *Lunch.* New York: Holt.

Goldstone, B. (1964). *The beastly feast.* New York: Holt.

Hoban, R. (1964). *Bread and jam for Frances.* New York: HarperTrophy.

Sharmat, M. (1989). *Gregory, the terrible eater.* New York: Scholastic.

Soto, G. (1995). *Chato's kitchen.* New York: Putnam.

Questions to Assess Students' Concept Sorts

1. _____ Was the student able to develop categories that included three or more pictures?
2. _____ Was the student able to sort all pictures into their categories?
3. _____ Was the student able to explain the categories or provide a label for them?
4. _____ Did the student set aside pictures that did not belong in these categories?
5. _____ Could the student sort in more than one way?

Extend

Ask students to take away all pictures that are not fruits or vegetables: "Leave your fruits and vegetables and take away all of the other pictures." Brainstorm other things that could go in each group. A discussion of the characteristics of fruits and vegetables can lead to language experiences with cutting and eating the fruits and vegetables. A number of sorts will come to students as they investigate the actual fruits: sorting by seeds, color, skin, ways we eat them, and so on.

Talk With, Write With, Read With

Create text to reread by collecting one-sentence dictations. Begin by talking about your favorite food and then ask students about theirs. Everyone likes to talk about food, so this topic is easy to discuss. After oral sharing ask students to dictate a sentence about something that is meaningful and familiar about their favorite foods. The dictations can be written individually or on a chart. For individual dictations, write the sentence at the bottom of a page and have the student draw a picture to accompany the sentence.

My favorite food is _____.

For a group chart collect several sentences, using students' names to identify their ideas. Each of the students' dictations would begin as follows:

[Student's Name] said, "My favorite food is _____."

Name _____   Date/Story Number_____

My Fruit

I peel, peel, peel my banana.

I cut, cut, cut my banana.

And I put the banana in a bowl.

I wash, wash, wash my apple.

I cut, cut, cut my apple.

And I put the apple in a bowl.

I peel, peel, peel my orange.

I cut, cut, cut my orange.

And I put the orange in a bowl.

SORT 1　Fruit/Not Fruit Concept Sort

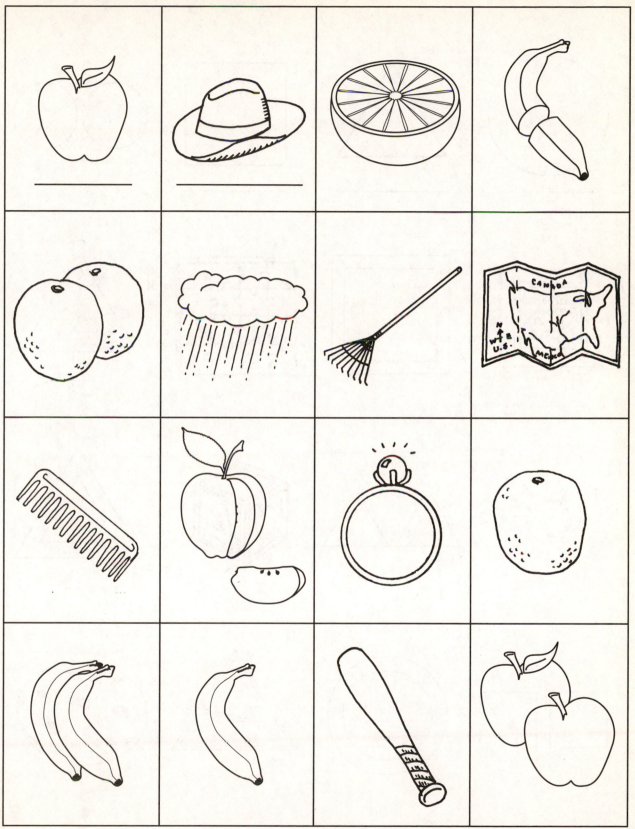

SORT 2A   Shapes: Circles, Triangles, and Squares Concept Sort

SORT 2B Shapes: Circles, Triangles, and Squares Concept Sort

Name _____   Date/Story Number _____

Circles

I make circles.

I make circles in the air.

I make circles on the paper.

I make circles on the board.

SORT 3   Part I: Animal/Not an Animal   Part II: Animal/Plant/Oddball

Name_____ Date _____ Number _____

Animals

Birds fly in the air.

Fish swim in the water.

And monkeys jump

Everywhere!

SORT 4   Clothes Concept Sort

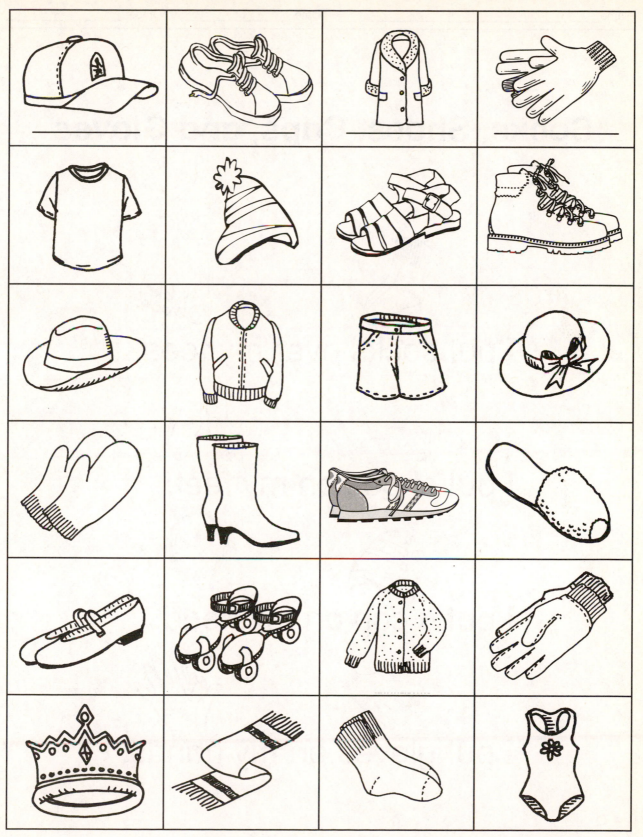

Name_____ Date _____ Number _____

Socks, Shoes, Caps, and Gloves

I put socks over my toes.

I put shoes on my feet.

I put a cap on my head.

I put gloves on my hands.

SORT 5 Cleaning Items Sort

Name_____ Date _____ Number _____

This Is the Way

This is the way we

wash our hands,

wash our hands,

wash our hands.

This is the way we

wash our hands

So early in the morning.

This Is the Way

This is the way we

_____ our_____ ,

_____ our_____ ,

_____ our_____ .

This is the way we

_____ our_____

So early in the morning.

SORT 6 Food Sort

Chapter 3   Phonological Awareness Picture Sorts

NOTES FOR THE TEACHER

In Chapter 4 of *Words Their Way* we describe phonological awareness as an umbrella term for a range of speech sounds beginning with rhyme and syllable awareness and extending to phonemic awareness—the ability to attend to, segment, or blend individual sounds within syllables. Teachers can direct attention to these sound units as they read to and with children, as they talk with children, and as they write with children. In this section we offer some lessons that focus on rhyme, syllables, and compound words. Phonemic awareness of beginning sounds or alliteration is addressed in the sorts for initial consonants.

Children's literature is the starting point for most of these lessons and we describe sample units that show how different parts of the emergent literacy diet can be developed around a core text. We hope you can find the titles we recommend, but if you cannot we hope that these lessons will serve as examples that will help you develop lessons based on your own favorite books. With or without the books, the sorts can be used to engage children in active exploration of rhyme and syllables.

Targeted Learners

Early emergent learners need to participate in phonological awareness activities that focus attention on syllables and rhyming words while middle to late emergent learners develop alliteration and rudimentary phonemic segmentation by sorting pictures that begin with the same sound. The spelling inventory will reveal how fully students are able to segment the sounds in a word. In the late emergent stage many children are able to identify at least one sound in a word, typically the first sound when it is salient, spelling *mat* as *M*.

The phonological awareness sorts in this chapter are most appropriate for students in the early emergent stage who were not successful in identifying the rhyming words on the Rhyme Identification assessment described in Chapter 1. However, even students who were successful at identifying rhyme and alliteration will enjoy these reading selections and sorts because rhyme, a poetic element, is so engaging. They will also benefit from the other literacy activities that go along with the books, songs, and rhymes. Students who were very successful at identifying rhyme might skip the rhyme sorts and do beginning sounds sorts. The particular activities you choose will depend on where students are developmentally.

Teaching Tips

There are three additional rhyme sorts and a bingo game on the *Words Their Way* CD-ROM that are ready to print out and use. There are many sources for additional

Literature Connection

Cole, J. (1989). *Anna Banana: 101 jump rope rhymes.* New York: Beech Tree Books.

Cole, J., & Calmenson, S. (1990). *Miss Mary Mack and other children's street rhymes.* New York: Beech Tree Books.

Glazer, T. (1973). *Eye winker, Tom tinker, chin chopper.* New York: Doubleday and Co.

Graham, C. (1994). *Mother Goose chants.* New York: Oxford University Press.

Merriam, E. (1994). *Higgle wiggle: Happy rhymes.* New York: Mulberry Books.

Nelson, E. L. (1981). *The silly songbook.* New York: Sterling Publishing Co., Inc.

Opie, I., & Wells, R. (1998). *My very first Mother Goose.* Cambridge, MA: Candlewick.

Prelutsky, J. (1983). *The Random House book of poetry for children.* New York: Random House.

Prelutsky, J. (1986). *Read aloud rhymes for the very young.* New York: Alfred A. Knopf.

Raffi. (1988). *Singable songbook.* New York: Knopf Books for Young Readers.

Raffi. (1990). *Shake my sillies out.* New York: Crown Publishers. And others in the Songs to Read Series.

poems, rhymes, songs, jingles, and finger plays, which are ways for children to respond to readings with hand signs and signals. We list a few in Literature Connection.

A student's native language or dialect may lead to alternate word pairings in a rhyme task. For example, students who speak Spanish may say that *rag* and *dog* rhyme. Ask students to read the pictures as they check, and this will give you a chance to hear if indeed they are said in the same manner.

STANDARD ROUTINES FOR PHONOLOGICAL AWARENESS

1. *Fill Students' Ears with the Sound of Rhyme.* Emergent learners need to have their ears filled with lots of rhymes before they will be able to identify rhymes, match rhymes, or create their own rhymes. Fortunately, the world of early childhood is filled with nursery rhymes, finger plays, songs, and stories written in rhyme, so there is lots of material to choose from. Make it a point to present a new rhyme or jingle every few days, especially those that can be sung as well as chanted. Reread and recite them many times and invite children to join in whenever possible.

2. *Teach Children the Concept of Rhyme and Syllables.* Oftentimes when you assess students' knowledge of rhyme they do poorly because they do not know what the term means. You not only need to fill their ears with rhyme, you need to explicitly teach what it is. Pause in your reading to identify rhyme, to allow children to supply a rhyming word, and to ask children to identify the rhymes. You don't need to find every rhyming word in a book, like *The Cat in the Hat* by Dr. Seuss, but pick out some of your favorites and ask the children for theirs. Write rhyming words you find in a story or poem on a chart and talk about how they sound alike at the end, at the same time you point to the common letters they share. Do the same thing with syllables. When you come to a long interesting word like *helicopter* take the time to talk about it: "Look at this long word. Let's say and clap the syllables in this word."

3. *Provide Rhyming Text for Read With Activities.* After learning a finger play, jingle, or song like *A-Hunting We Will Go*, transcribe three to six lines of the text on a large chart, sentence strips, whiteboard, PowerPoint, transparency, or similar method, to create predictable and memorable reading material for emergent readers. Model how to point to each word as you read it aloud and give students their own copy so they can read along and point to the words as well. It is by pointing to memorized text that students begin to develop a concept of word in print and come to understand the alphabetic principle at work. Find the rhyming words in the text and highlight or underline them. Show students how words of two or more syllables require more than one touch as they track print. See Chapter 6 of this book for more ideas about developing a student's concept of word through Read With activities in class and at home, using saved selections in personal readers as described on page 168.

4. *Create Rhyming Sorts.* In this chapter we will provide some examples of rhyming sorts, but you can create your own using pictures from the collection in *Words Their Way*. There is a list of rhyming pictures in the Appendix that you can put in sets for sorts. You can also download images or use picture cards you may have in your classroom. What is important is that children get lots of practice with their own set of pictures or in centers after the vocabulary has been introduced (critical for English learners) and the sort has been modeled in a group.

5. *Create Games.* Rhyming Bingo or Rhyming Concentration, described in *Words Their Way*, are easy to create and play. They follow the traditional rules and format as Bingo or Concentration and once you teach children how the game works it can be adapted for other features, such as Alphabet Bingo. Of course there are many commercially available games and software that will reinforce a sense of rhyme.

6. *Model Phonological Awareness While You Write with Children.* Whenever you write in front of children you have the opportunity to model how speech can be slowed down and broken into units. Begin by breaking a sentence into words. "We are going to write *'Today is Friday.'* Let's count how many words we need to write." Then break words into syllables: "*Today* has two syllables, *to-day*. Let's start by spelling *to*." Finally break words into phonemes, stretching them out when you can or emphasizing the sounds with repetition: "What is the first sound in *to*? Listen: *t-t-t-t-oo*. Do you hear the /t/ sound at the beginning?"

RHYME

Oh, A-Hunting We Will Go

Read To: Literature Link

Oh, A-Hunting We Will Go is based on a traditional song available in a picture book adapted and illustrated by John Langstaff (1991). It has a simple predictable rhyme that offers an easy introduction to matching rhyming pairs. The activities below start with the book, but could be used with just the words of the song if you do not have the book. The traditional song goes like this:

Oh, A-Hunting We Will Go

Oh, a-hunting we will go,
A-hunting we will go.
We'll catch a fox
and put him in a box
and then we'll let him go.

Various animals are substituted for the fox, such as a mouse who is put in a house and a goat who is put in a boat. You may want to begin by teaching children the song. You can find copies of the traditional verses by searching the Web under the title of the song both with and without the word *Oh*.

Introduce the book by looking at the cover and talking about the title. Talk about what the children might be hunting for. Read the book aloud, pausing to give children a chance to supply the rhyming words after the first few pages. Talk about the words that rhyme and go back through the book to name the rhyming pairs, using the pictures as clues. Read the book a second time and encourage the children to read along with you as you point to the words. Children in kindergarten should be successful at reading the book from memory with the support of the pictures.

Read With: *Oh, A-Hunting We Will Go*

Create an enlarged copy of the first verse of the song by copying the words onto a chart or making an overhead transparency of page 68 so children can easily see the words as they recite or sing. Make a copy of page 68 for each child as well so that he or she can follow along with their finger as they read from memory. The hyphenated *A-hunting* is likely to get them off track right at the beginning so model how to point to that part. Talk about how the words *fox* and *box* rhyme and show children how to underline them or highlight them. Children can illustrate this part of the song and add it to a personal reader (described in Chapter 6). We encourage you to make sentence strips of the lines for children to rebuild in a pocket chart, leaving the last word in lines 3 and 4 blank, as on page 69. That way you can insert different words or the pictures provided on page 70 in the blank spaces to change the verses.

Rhyme Sort 7

Prepare a copy of the rhyming picture sort on page 70 that features some of the animals and places where they can be put. Model the sort by setting out all the pictures and selecting the *fox*. Explain: "Here is a picture of the fox. What word rhymes with *fox*? I am going to put the fox and the box together." Explain that *fox* and *box* rhyme because they end with the same sounds. Continue with each animal, pairing them up with the places in which they are put, in columns that will look like this:

fox	box
goat	boat
whale	pail
mouse	house
snake	cake
fish	dish

As a group, name each pictured pair. Mix up the pictures and have the children match under your direction. To make the matching easier you can put together three pictures, two that rhyme and one that does not (e.g., *fox*, *dish*, and *box*), and ask a child to select the two that rhyme. This "odd man out" approach narrows the number of choices for children who are first learning to make rhyming matches. You can expect some confusion if children have been doing concept sorts or sorting by beginning sound, so model carefully and explain why you are sorting as you do.

Sort, Check, and Reflect

Make a copy of the blackline master for each student. Students can use a distinct color crayon to quickly scribble on the back side of their paper before cutting it apart. This helps prevent cards from getting mixed up among students sitting near each other.

Help children cut out their pictures and tell them to sort the same way as you did in the group. As you move around to check the children's work, encourage them to name the rhyming pairs. Ask them to tell you how the words in each pair are alike (e.g., they rhyme, they end with the same sound). Save the pictures in an envelope or plastic bag to sort again over several days and to create the book described below.

Extend with Frame Sentences

Help children create their own books by pasting each rhyming pair from their sorting collection onto a copy of page 69 with the following frame sentence: *"We'll catch a* _____ *and put him in a* _____ *and then we'll let him go."* Children can use their own invented spelling to fill in the blanks or you can do the writing for them. Children will need three pages to accommodate all the rhyming pictures. These can be cut in half and stapled to make a book.

Children should be encouraged to create their own verses using other animals, such as *sheep in a jeep, moose in a caboose, frog on a log, cat* or *rat in a hat, bee in a tree, llamas in pajamas,* and so on. They can illustrate these and add them to their book.

Alphabet Hunt

For students still learning the alphabet, use the text to go on a letter hunt. Ask children to find particular letters in the text and point to them. "Who can find the letter *w*, the first letter in *we*?" Students might underline, circle, or highlight these letters on a copy of the song.

Letter–Sound Sorts

Beginning sound sorts are appropriate for students in the middle to late emergent stage: Select words like *fox* and *box* as key words to develop a beginning sound sort as described in Chapter 5.

Word Recognition

There are many high-frequency words that children in the late emergent stage can learn from this song: *we, will, and, go, him, in, then, let.* They make good candidates, along with the names of animals, to add to a word bank or word wall described in Chapter 6.

Here Are My Hands

Read To: Literature Link

The names for the parts of the human body are part of our basic vocabulary and are learned early on when we learn a language. Many books for young children feature body parts, but *Here Are My Hands* by Bill Martin and John Archambault (1987) presents them in a simple rhyming format along with a multicultural cast of characters that makes the book especially appealing. Introduce the book by looking at the cover and talking about the title. Read the book aloud. On a second reading students may be able to supply the rhyming word if you pause after the first sentence of each rhyming set.

Rhyme Sort 8

Prepare a copy of the rhyming picture sort on page 71 that features body parts and display all the cut-out pictures. Begin by asking the students to help you find and name all the parts of a body. Explain that two of the body parts rhyme (*toes* and *nose*) and name the pictures to find them. Put *toes* under *nose*. Continue with *nose* by saying "What else rhymes with *nose*? Let's name the other pictures and listen for words that rhyme with *nose*." Find the *hose* and the *rose* and place them under *nose*. Repeat with the other body parts, involving the children as much as possible. The final sort will look something like this:

Nose	Knees	Hair	Head
toes	keys	bear	bed
hose	cheese	pear	bread
rose	trees	chair	

As a group, name the pictures in each column and talk about how they are alike—they all rhyme. Mix up the pictures and have the children sort under your direction. Use "odd man out" to support children who might struggle with finding a rhyme from so many choices. Ask students to name the pictures in each row and support English language learners as they acquire the new vocabulary.

Sort, Check, and Reflect

Give each child a copy of their own pictures to cut apart and sort, using the body parts for headers. As you move around to check the children's work, encourage them to name the rhyming words and talk about how the words in each pair are alike. Resort over several days as seatwork or in centers.

Extend

See if children can come up with words that rhyme with other body parts as you revisit the book or as children touch and name other parts of their body. You might play a game that goes like this: "Can you touch a part of your body that rhymes with *tears*?" (ears) "With *pin*?" (chin). Here are some other suggestions: *farm/arm, band/hand, cries/eyes, zip/lip* or *hip, peek/cheek, peck/neck, list/wrist, seat/feet, stands/hands, egg/leg,* or *buckle/knuckle.* Repeat this many times until children get good at it.

Teach children the traditional jingle *Eenie Meenie Minee Moe* in which we try to catch a tiger by the toe. Substitute different nonsense words for *moe* and see if students can figure out the body part as in:

Eenie meenie miney mose   Eenie meenie miney mail   Eenie meenie miney meg
Catch a tiger by the nose.   Catch a tiger by the tail.   Catch a tiger by the leg.

Letter–Sound Sorts

As noted previously, beginning sound sorts are appropriate for students in the middle to late emergent stage. In this case, select words like *hand* and *nose* as key words to develop a beginning sound sort.

Read With: *Open and Close*

Many books and jingles on body parts are available to read with your children, and some of them are simple enough to be read from memory by emergent readers. On page 72 is a simple poem that can be written on a chart or prepared as a handout. Students enjoy reading this text to each other, directing others to follow the movements as they read. Students open and close their hands, eyes, and mouths several times as they read the last line. Model how to point to the two-syllable word *open* to help students without a concept of word learn to point accurately.

Open and Close

Hands open.	Mouths open.
Hands close.	Mouths close.
Eyes open.	Open and close,
Eyes close.	Here we go.

Write With

There are many possibilities for writing with children as follow-ups. Have children brainstorm other things that they do with their hands or feet and record their dictations on a chart that can be reread together. You can use a simple sentence frame such as shown in the following paragraph, which is especially helpful for English learners. Model segmenting the sounds, isolating a sound, and representing the sound with a letter as you write for them. Encourage the students to point to the words as they reread the sentences. Both hands and feet can be traced and cut out with students' ideas written on them by the teacher, or handprints and footprints can be used to illustrate their ideas.

My _____ open. (*eyes, hands, toes, mouth*)
My _____ close.

"I Can't," Said the Ant

Read To: Literature Link

In the picture book *"I Can't," Said the Ant* by Polly Cameron (1961), ants and spiders work together to return a teapot to the kitchen counter after it falls to the floor. There are lots of rhyming pairs, and we offer you three different rhyming sorts to use with or without the book.

Begin by reading the book aloud, pausing to give children a chance to supply the rhyming words cued by the picture. Be selective. Children will recognize many of the objects, but some, like *artichoke, trout*, and *thyme,* will not be familiar to most. Just supply those and keep going. On a second reading you may want to stop and talk with your children about some of these new words. The text for this book is too long and complicated to expect children to read along with you, but you can select three to five sentences to put on a chart or sentence strips along with a picture to cue the rhyme.

Rhyme Sort 9A

The rhyming picture sorts we supply on pages 73, 74, and 75 begin with some of the kitchen objects cited in the book. Prepare the first set of pictures for modeling. Lay out *clock, fly, pie,* and *pan* for the children to see and name each one. Read aloud the sentence from the book that each came from, letting the children identify the rhyming word. Arrange these pictures in a row. Say, "*Pie* and *fly*—those words rhyme. I am going to put *pie* under *fly* because they sound alike at the end." Move the pie under the fly. Put out the remaining pictures. Explain that there are more words that rhyme with each of these pictures. Model several and then sort the rest with student help. Leave the headers up and scramble the rest of the pictures. Give a picture to each child in the group to sort under the correct header. The sort will look something like this:

clock	fly	pan
block	pie	van
rock	cry	can
sock	eye	man
lock	tie	fan

Sort, Check, and Reflect

Give each child a copy of their own pictures to cut apart and sort for rhyming pairs. As you move around to check the children's work, encourage them to name the rhyming words in each column. Ask them to tell you how the words are alike (e.g., they rhyme, they end with the same sound). Save the pictures to sort again over several days. Pair up English learners with English speakers to support their pronunciation and sorting.

Rhyme Sorts 9B and 9C

Introduce the other two rhyming sorts in the same way. Have the students sort them over several days. Try putting two and then three sets together for a grand rhyming sort.

bug	mop	beet		jar	plate	bell	grape
rug	top	feet		car	gate	well	tape
plug	shop	seat		star	skate	shell	cape
hug	pop	street					

Extend

Rhyming Bingo is available on the *Words Their Way* CD-ROM to print out and would make a good follow-up game. Rhyming Concentration, described in *Words Their Way,* is also a good game to introduce here.

Brainstorm more rhyming words for each category. (These might include words like *tell* or *late* that cannot be pictured, but are words that children would know.) You can also create sentences similar to the ones in the story. Here are some examples:

"What a bug," said the rug.
"Don't stare," said the chair.
"Use the mat," said the cat.
"I've got to run," said the bun.

Children can glue the pictures that rhyme together. You might create a rhyming book for each child by folding several sheets of paper and gluing a different set of rhyming pictures on each page.

Rhyming Picture Sorts
with Bruce Mcmillan Books

Read To: Literature Link

In *One Sun: A Book of Terse Verse* author and photographer Bruce McMillan (1990) creates the simplest of rhyme books using two-word "hink pinks" that describe a day at the beach. *Play Day* (1992) is a similar book by McMillan, and either or both of these books can be used to introduce these rhyming sorts. Although this book is currently out of print you can probably find it in a library or purchase used copies online.

Begin by reading the book(s) aloud, pausing to give children a chance to supply the rhyming words cued by the picture (when they are likely to be successful). On a second reading you may want to stop and talk with your children about any new words. The text for these books is so simple that children can easily pick it up and read it with the support of the pictures, the rhymes, and their memories, so leave the book out for children to use on their own.

Rhyme Sorts 10A and 10B

The rhyming picture sort on page 76 features some of the rhyming pairs from the books. Prepare a set of pictures for modeling and display all of the pictures. Challenge your students to find rhyming pairs. If they have difficulty, narrow the choices with the "odd man out" strategy. The words for these pictures are shown in the following list:

sand	whale	bear	toe	duck	cub
hand	pail	chair	bow	truck	tub

A second sort, on page 77, capitalizes on the many color rhymes featured in the two books. Make a copy of the sort and color in the spaces as indicated with crayons or markers. The pairs will be as shown here.

tan	brown	pink	green	white	blue
man	crown	drink	bean	kite	shoe

Sort, Check, and Reflect

Give each child a copy of their own pictures to color, cut apart, and sort for rhyming pairs. As you move around to check the children's work, encourage them to name the rhyming words. Think of other color pairs like *red bed, yellow jello, black backpack,* or *gray day.*

Extend

Many teachers and children have created their own terse verse books using pictures that they have taken around the school building. Here are some possible hink pinks to find, create, photograph, and label. You and your children can think of more.

scream team	bear chair	two drew	new shoe	art cart
bright light	twin grin	grass class	sad lad	play clay
ball hall or	eight date (on	far car	school rule	
ball wall	calendar)			

Assessment for Rhyme

Observe informally as students respond in groups and sort individually to assess their developing sense of rhyme. After several weeks of working on rhyme you may want to use the assessment on page 17 as a posttest. Expect that it will take time and lots of practice for some children to master this concept so continue to include the weekly routines described earlier. There are some additional rhyme sorts on the *Words Their Way* CD-ROM and on pages 129 and 197 in this book.

SYLLABLES

Notes for the Teacher

Segmenting words into syllables is one aspect of phonological awareness that comes fairly easily to children. While rhymes and phonemes are abstract and depend on knowing what to pay attention to, syllables are concrete. We can physically sense syllables because each one is a separate pulse of air through the mouth. We can split words into syllables and leave clear spaces between them without distorting the sounds. Children can learn to tap them, clap them, or indicate them in other motoric ways that do not work readily for any other phonological elements. What children do not know is what those rhythmic units might be called and why we would want to pay attention to them.

You can call them *beats, taps,* or *claps* but we see no reason to avoid calling them what they are—*syllables.* Draw children's attention to them when you read aloud and talk about them when you write for children. When you write for and with children, model how you can break a long word like *Saturday* into syllables before writing the letters for each sound.

Start with Children's Names

Write the name of each child in the class on pieces of tagboard. Write short names on short pieces about 3 × 4 and longer names on pieces about 3 × 10. Write the numerals 1 through 4 on tagboard and use them to create headers in a pocket chart. Select a two-syllable name like *Jose* and say it as you tap the card twice, once for each syllable. Explain to the children that there are two syllables in the name. Say the name again and have children clap the beats. Then put the name under the numeral two. Select a name with three syllables like *Amanda,* clap the syllables, and place it under the numeral three. Then select a one-syllable name. Continue to clap the syllables in everyone's name and sort them accordingly. After all the names are sorted, read down each column of names after saying something like "Let's read the names that have one syllable." Leave the names and key pictures in the pocket chart so that children can sort them again on their own. If you have digital pictures of the children you could create a master set by gluing the pictures on a template provided in the Appendix. You will find many uses for these pictures, including giving each child a sheet to cut apart for sorting by syllables.

The Very Hungry Caterpillar

Read To: Literature Link

Read *The Very Hungry Caterpillar* by Eric Carle (1971) prior to doing this sort. Introduce the book by looking at the cover and talking about the title. Read the book aloud, pausing to give children a chance to supply the words cued by the pictures. You might want to make sentence strips of the lines that feature the days of the week and the different foods the caterpillar eats each day and put them into a pocket chart for Read With activities. Teach vocabulary (e.g., *plums*) that might be unfamiliar to the children.

Select some words from the story such as *hungry, caterpillar, very, butterfly, Monday, stomachache, Saturday,* and so on to model how the syllables in words can be separated as we talk and can be clapped or tapped. Say something like "Listen as I say this word: *hun-gry.*" Say it again as you clap along or tap your foot for each syllable. Invite the children to clap or tap along with you. Explain that words can be broken into syllables and continue to do this with several more words such as *beautiful, salami, cupcake, chocolate,* and *Sunday.*

Syllable Sort 11A

Prepare a copy of the sort on page 78, which features some of the one- and two-syllable words from the book. Model the sort by setting out all the pictures and putting the numerals as headers. Explain, "Here is an apple. Listen, *apple* has two syllables, *ap-ple.* Clap the syllables with me: *ap-ple.* I am going to put this picture under the number two because it has two syllables." Repeat with a one-syllable picture such as the plum. Explain that it has only one syllable and put it under the numeral one. Involve the children in sorting the rest of the pictures, clapping the syllables for each one. After sorting all of them, check the sort by reading all the one-syllable words and then the two-syllable words.

1·	2··
plum	apple
leaf	sausage
pear	pickle
cheese	cupcake
pie	cherries

Sort, Check, and Reflect

Give each child a copy of their own pictures to cut apart and sort by number of syllables. As you move around to check the children's work, encourage them to clap or tap the syllables. Ask them to tell you how the words in each column are alike.

Syllable Sort 11B

On another day prepare a copy of the sort on page 79, which features some of the longer words from the book as well as some additional words. Identify any pictures you think your students might not know, such as *helicopter*. Demonstrate how to sort several words in a manner similar to the first sort before inviting the children to join in with you.

3···	4::	5:·:
butterfly	caterpillar	refrigerator
lollipop	watermelon	hippopotamus
banana	alligator	
hamburger	helicopter	
strawberry	motorcycle	

Extend

Combine the two-, three-, four-, and five-syllable pictures when students are sorting accurately and fluently. Continue to look for words with two, three, and four syllables in other books and clap them. Children can look through magazines for pictures to add to their sorts.

Return to familiar readings to hunt for words by the number of syllables. Skip the single-syllable words and focus on two-, three-, and four-syllable words.

Use objects and pictures from concept sorts and categorize them by the number of syllables. The names of locations in your area such as streets, cities, schools, and states are a fine source of polysyllabic words.

Concept Sort

Ask the students if they can think of other ways to sort the pictures. They can separate the foods from the nonfoods. Another sort can be things that grow (living things) and things that don't grow (nonliving things).

Write With

It is fun to create variations of this popular storybook. After creating a group dictation together using different names, students can fill in a frame sentence and create their own little books, adding the illustrations. One suggestion is to focus on days of the week, numbers, and children's food preferences in sentences such as these:

On Monday Lisa ate one banana.
On Tuesday Lisa ate two apples.

Compound Cupcakes

Notes for the Teacher

Phonological awareness includes an awareness of breaking and blending word parts that can be first explored in the creation of compound words. At this point it is not important for students to learn the term "compound word." Instead, you can talk about putting two words together to make a big word or taking a big word apart. As children work with these words they also have the opportunity to refine or expand their vocabulary because meaning is explored as well.

Sorts 12A and 12B: Compound Words

The word *cupcake* is an easy compound word to introduce this sort. Make a copy of the sort on page 80 for modeling. Find the picture of the cup, the cake, and the cupcake. Hold up the cup in one hand and the cake in the other and name each, "Here is a cup. Here is a cake." Push the pictures together and add the picture of the cupcake. Explain, "When I put *cup* and *cake* together I have a new word, *cupcake*!" Continue to model how you put the rest of the words together. Then reverse the process. Hold up a picture of a compound word such as *skateboard* and say, "Can we say this as two words? *Skate board*. Let's find the two words that go together to make *skateboard*." Place the compound word first and then the skate and board pictures.

cup	cake	cupcake
dog	house	doghouse
foot	ball	football
snow	man	snowman
skate	board	skateboard

A second set of pictures on page 81 is included to use for another lesson. When students can do it easily combine the two sorts and match up all ten compound words. The second set is as follows:

lip	stick	lipstick
finger	nail	fingernail
sun	glasses	sunglasses
rain	coat	raincoat
mail	box	mailbox

Sort, Check, and Reflect

Make a copy of the pictures for students to match up independently. As you go around to check students' work ask them to name the two pictures first and then the compound word that they form.

Literature Connection

Hambleton, L., & Turhan, S. (2007). *Strawberry bullfrog: Fun with compound words.* Chicago: Milet Publishing.

Trattles, P. (2005). *Flying butter* (Rookie Readers). New York: Scholastic.

Walton, R. (2005). *Once there was a bull-frog.* Layton, UT: Gibbs Smith.

Extend

Repeat this activity orally by saying the following words and asking students to say the words that make up the compound. Reverse the process by saying the individual words and asking students to say the compound word. Children might be asked to choose a word and illustrate it. You can pose riddles such as, "I am thinking of a word that has *sand* and *box*." Clap the syllables in the larger words like *pocketbook, newspaper, basketball,* and so on. Children might draw their own pictures to illustrate some of these.

lighthouse	sandbox	basketball
pocketbook	cowboy	hairbrush
starfish	fireman	pigpen
pancake	goldfish	popcorn
butterfly	doorbell	treetop
handbag	ladybug	rainbow

Name_____ Date _____ Number _____

Oh, A-Hunting We Will Go

Oh, a-hunting we will go,

A-hunting we will go.

We'll catch a fox,

and put him in a box,

and then we'll let him go.

We'll catch a _____
and put him in a _____
and then we'll let him go.

Frame Sentences for Cut-and-Paste Book

Name _____   Date/Story Number_____

We'll catch a _____
and put him in a _____
and then we'll let him go.

We'll catch a _____
and put him in a _____
and then we'll let him go.

SORT 8 Rhyming with Body Part Pictures

71

Open and Close

Hands open.

Hands close.

Eyes open.

Eyes close.

Mouths open.

Mouths close.

Open and close,

Here we go!

SORT 9A   Rhyming Sort for "I Can't," Said the Ant

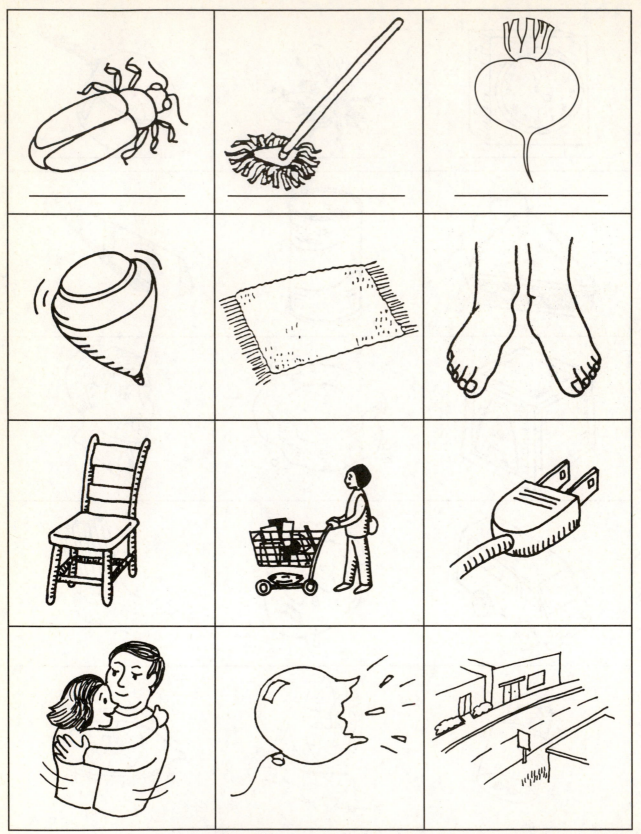

SORT 9C Rhyming Sort for "I Can't," Said the Ant

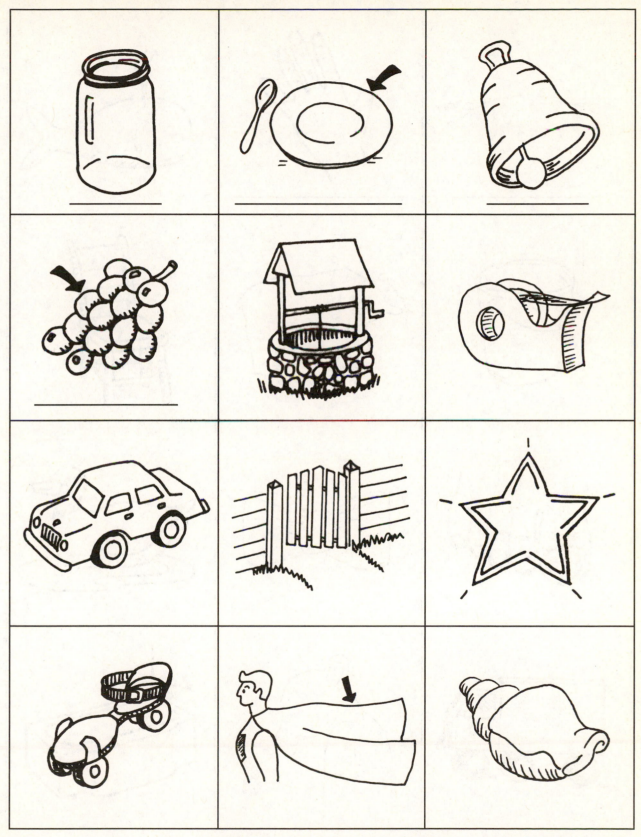

SORT 11A How Many Syllables Can You Count?

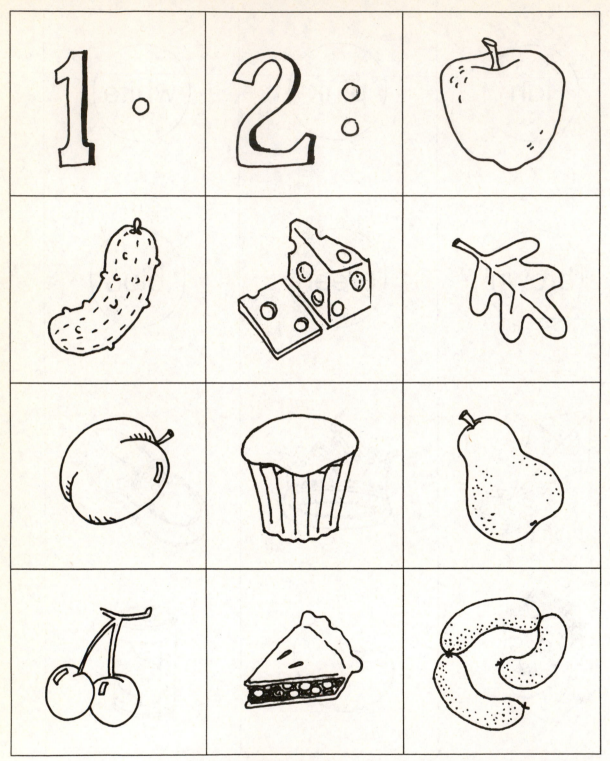

SORT 11B   How Many Syllables Can You Count?

SORT 12A   Compound Words

SORT 12B Compound Words

Chapter 4   Alphabet Knowledge

NOTES FOR THE TEACHER

Background

There is much to learn about the alphabet: names, sequence, capital and lowercase forms, font variations, and how to write them. See Chapter 4 in *Words their Way* for a full discussion of alphabet learning. In this section we describe daily routines that help children learn their letters and an example of how a core book is used for Read With, Write With, Talk With, and Word Study activities. There is also an alphabet tracking strip, letters to use for sequencing and matching, and capital and lowercase letters across a variety of font styles. It is not the case that you will devote several weeks to learning the alphabet using these materials and then move on to other features. The study of the alphabet should be an integral part of daily literacy activities for emergent learners over a long period of time, as reflected by the suggestions and reminders we offer throughout this book.

Targeted Learners

Assess your students' knowledge of the alphabet using the resources in the first chapter of this book or similar tools. From these you should gather information about how well they can recite the alphabet and identify uppercase and lowercase forms. Then plan your instruction according to what you find. The form on page 92 can be used to keep a record of those they know. You might write the date each is acquired.

1. Students who know few letters will benefit from all the activities described in this section and should study all the letters in both upper- and lowercase forms. A good starting place may be the activities *Start with Children's Names* and *One Child's Name* described in *Words Their Way*. These activities personalize the alphabet and help children make connections between letters and the important people in their lives. They will need lots of practice singing the song and reciting the letters of the alphabet paired with tracking the letters on an alphabet strip. Reassess students on all letters after eight or nine weeks. Add to the assessment form on page 92.

2. Students who know about half of their letters will also benefit from a general study of the alphabet, but targeted instruction is also recommended. Identify the letters that present the most problems and plan activities for these. For example, you might create an Alphabet Spin game with the letters *Bb, Dd, Pp,* and *Qq* to provide extra practice for letters frequently confused. Letters will receive attention during other literacy activities such as writing and the study of beginning consonants. Assess again after eight or nine weeks.

3. Students who know most of their letters at the beginning of kindergarten will probably pick up the few that they do not know in the course of daily talk about letters

that should accompany Read To and Read With lessons, writing, and the study of beginning sounds. These students may still benefit from the font sorts because they may not recognize the letters across a variety of print styles but will not need the other activities designed to just learn letter identification. Assess again only those letters they missed.

4. Students who know all the letters in both upper- and lowercase forms should study letter–sound correspondences based on the results of the spelling inventory. They may be in the letter name–alphabetic stage and do not need to study the alphabet directly. Some of these students may still reverse lowercase *b, d, p,* and *q* but can quickly correct themselves when prompted.

Teaching Tips

If you use the computer to create alphabet materials such as games or if you type up dictations or other materials that students will read, think carefully about the font you choose. Century Gothic and Comic Sans MS are two fonts available in Microsoft Word that are very similar to the manuscript taught to young children and presented on alphabet charts. Once students know most of their letters then you might use a font style much like the type in this book, where lowercase *a*s and *g*s are distinctly different. Students need to learn these variations but not at first.

In most other English-speaking countries the letter *Z* is named "zed," not "zee." Keep this in mind when you are assessing students who might have learned the alphabet in another country.

For English learners the English alphabet may be completely new. Therefore, it is important to provide instructional support strategies such as visuals, hands-on materials, and meaningful projects. The collection of sorts and learning activities in this section will help you make learning the letters in English fun, active, and relevant to students' lives. Research other alphabets online to find commonalities and differences. The Vietnamese alphabet, for example, has many of the same consonants but lacks *F, J, W,* and *Z.*

STANDARD ROUTINES FOR LEARNING THE ALPHABET

1. *Sing the Alphabet Song Regularly.* Singing the ABC song (every day in preschool and early kindergarten) is usually children's first introduction to learning about the alphabet. Although it is a valuable introduction, children may not actually know that it contains references to individual letters. *LMNOP* becomes a phrase. It is important to point to the letters on a chart or alphabet strip, which means slowing down the *LMNOP* part. Look for recordings of the alphabet song that offer some variations. You may find some engaging versions on YouTube and other Internet sources by searching "alphabet song."

2. *Lead Children in Reciting the Letters of the Alphabet.* Pair recitation with pointing and give students their own alphabet strip or the alphabet tracking strip we provide on page 95. Keep a copy of the alphabet displayed where children can see it, but even more important, give students a copy they can have where they sit to write or draw.

3. *Create an Alphabet Scrapbook.* A personal alphabet scrapbook is easy to make and can be added to all year as students learn new information about letters. Seven sheets of heavy paper folded and stapled will make enough pages and a cover also. The first activity can be pasting a capital and lowercase letter on each page;

resources in this chapter can be used for that. Students can add letters that they find in newspapers and magazines or paste in the letters from the font sorts. Classmates' names can be added. As they study beginning sounds they can draw or paste in pictures to go with the letters. And finally, words can be added to create a beginning dictionary. Of course you can also have students work collaboratively on pages for a class alphabet book.

4. *Letter Hunts.* Sometimes you can ask students to find and point to letters you name on a strip or on a chart, or you can point and ask for the name. Show them how to recite the alphabet to find a letter they might not recognize. This is particularly valuable for students who might know most letters and need to focus on just a few. You can pair up students to quiz each other. You can also send students on a letter hunt through the classroom checking bulletin boards, calendars, posters, and so on. Each time they find a letter they can write it on a notecard or whiteboard. Other letter hunts can be through magazines, junk mail, catalogs, or a newspaper where students can highlight the featured letter with a marker or cut it out and paste it on a chart. This is valuable as a way to introduce a variety of font styles.

5. *Model Writing with Children.* Take advantage of every opportunity to model for children how to use the alphabet to write. In Chapter 4 of *Words Their Way* we describe the Morning Message activity as one example of interactive writing. You will write with your students when you make lists, record dictations, compose thank you notes, and so on. Show students how you identify the letter needed to represent a sound, refer to the alphabet chart to see what a letter looks like, and demonstrate how to form the letter. Call on students to find a particular letter needed for writing on a chart or their own alphabet strip. This will help students understand the importance of memorizing all those letters—they are needed to communicate.

6. *Point Out Letters.* The world is full of letters, but students may not always pay attention to them. Point out letters on signs like the X in *exit*. Talk about the unusual shape that lowercase *g* takes in most printed material. Note how capital letters may be used to show emphasis, as in "STOP!" Help students learn to use letters as a guide for guessing the titles of books. If you know that certain students need to learn particular letters, ask them to point to that letter in a book title, in a poem displayed on a chart, and so forth.

7. *Share Alphabet Books.* Alphabet books are full of humor and imaginative artwork that fascinate and engage children as they teach both letter names and letter sounds. *Words Their Way* has a list of titles that we especially like and other recommended titles are listed on page 86; there are hundreds of others to choose from and more every year. Present alphabet books in an interactive fashion to involve students in naming the letters and objects they see on the page. Leave them out for students to revisit on their own. When students are studying beginning consonant sounds teach them how to use alphabet books as a reference to find other things that begin with a targeted letter.

8. *Provide Alphabet Games and Puzzles.* An alphabet center should be ongoing all year in both preschool and kindergarten classrooms. There are many commercially prepared games and puzzles that young children will enjoy working on independently, and you can also make many yourself. Alphabet Eggs and Alphabet Spin are some of the favorites described in *Words Their Way* and available on the CD-ROM to print out. Others include Alphabet Concentration, Alphabet Cereal Sort, and the *Chicka Chicka Boom Boom* sort. Change puzzles and games on a regular basis to keep children coming back for more.

Literature Connection

Here are some alphabet books we recommend; more are listed in *Words Their Way.*

Ada, A. F., & Simon, S. (1997). *Gathering the sun: An alphabet in Spanish and English.* Boston: Lothrop Publishing.

Ehlert, L. (1989). *Eating the alphabet: Fruits and vegetables from A to Z.* San Diego: Harcourt Brace.

Fleming, D. (2006). *Alphabet under construction.* New York: Henry Holt & Co.

Isadora, R. (2001). *ABC pop!* New York: Puffin.

Johnson, S. T. (1999). *Alphabet city.* New York: Puffin.

Lobel, A. (1989). *On Market Street.* New York: HarperTrophy.

MacDonald, R. (2003). *Achoo! Bang! Crash! The noisy alphabet.* Brookfield, CT: Roaring Brook Press.

MacDonald, S. (2005). *Alphabatics.* New Yorks: Aladdin.

Miranda, A. (2001). *Alphabet fiesta.* New York: Turtle Books.

Sendak, M. (1990). *Alligators all around: An alphabet book.* New York: Harper and Row.

Wormell, C. (2004). *The new alphabet of animals.* Philadelphia: Running Press Kids.

CHICKA CHICKA BOOM BOOM

Chicka Chicka Boom Boom by Bill Martin and John Archambault (1989) is a favorite alphabet book because it features a cast of characters that includes the lowercase adventurous kids who must be comforted by the capital letter mamas, papas, uncles, and aunts when they fall out of the coconut tree. It provides a good example of how you can use a core book as the starting point for a variety of integrated literacy activities. Animated versions of the story may be found on CDs or the Internet. The following ideas provide several ways to share the story and integrate a number of literacy skills. You can find more suggestions and story extensions by searching online under the title of the book.

Read To

Talk about the cover of the book and the illustration of a coconut tree. It might remind some children of palm trees. Since many children may never have seen a coconut you might get one at the supermarket to show and later break it open for a language experience described below under Talk With. Sing or recite the alphabet, pointing to the letters on the inside cover. Point out that each letter has a capital and lowercase form. Explain that this is a story about what happens to the lowercase letters. Read the story through, enjoying the rollicking rhyme and illustrations and stopping to make predictions about what might happen next. Do a second reading and encourage children to identify the letters and join in on the lines that repeat.

Read With

Make a chart or sentence strips of page 93. "Chicka chicka boom boom, Will there be enough room? Here comes _____ up the coconut tree." Model how to point to the words, especially the two- and three-syllable words like *chicka*, *enough*, and *coconut* (clap the syllables in these words). Students can take turns reading the chart with different letters substituted in the blank space. Make a copy of the text for each student, leaving enough space to illustrate it. Students can select their favorite letter to write in the space and should practice reading the lines as they point to practice tracking. An alternative would be to insert students' names for the letter as in "Here comes Travis up the coconut tree."

Alphabet Study

Dump a collection of plastic letters on the rug (or copy and cut apart the letters on pages 96 and 97). Talk about how the letters are all mixed up and need to be put in order. Reread the story and call on children to find the letters as they are named. Then work together as a group to sequence them. Put the letters in the alphabet center so students can repeat this activity independently or in small groups. Include both capital and lowercase letters for matching both forms. See Chapter 4 in *Words Their Way* for ideas about creating a "boom board" for matching capitals and lowercase letters and a coconut tree for acting out the story.

Rhyming Letter Sort 13

Reread the story, pausing at the end of a sentence where rhyme and familiarity will help children supply the word: "Chicka chicka boom boom, Will there be enough _____?" Identify and record the rhyming words on a chart: "*Boom* and *room* are rhyming words. We will add them to our list."

Reread the selection and talk about how any letter can be substituted in the blank space but only certain letters will rhyme with *tree*. Go through all the letters and help students sort them with your guidance into those that rhyme with *tree* (*b, c, d, e, g, p, t, v, z*) and those that do not (*a, f, h, i, j,* etc.).

Give all students a copy of the alphabet sort on page 94. Model the sort first by naming the four pictures to use as headers. Then explain that the rest of the letters will be sorted under the picture that rhymes. Hold up a letter (*J*, for example) and say, "Here is the letter *J* (both capital and lowercase). I want to find the picture that rhymes with *J*. *J–tree, J–tray, J–pie, J–shoe. J* and *tray* rhyme so I will put it under the tray." Model several more and then ask students to help you sort the rest. Make a copy of the same sort for children to cut up and practice with a partner or independently. Since not all your students will know all of the letters let them work in groups to do this. The final sort will look something like this:

Tree	Tray	Pie	Shoe
Bb, Dd, Ee,	Aa, Jj, Kk	Ii, Yy	Qq, Uu, Ww
Cc, Gg, Pp,			
Tt, Vv, Zz			

Concept Sort

Lay out a collection of letters using plastic letters, tiles, or letter cards. Brainstorm with students how they might sort them in different ways. One sort might be letters with curved lines (*O, C, D*), letters with slanted lines (*M, Y, Z*), and letters with just straight lines (*I, T, L*). Another sort might be letters that look the same in both upper and lowercase forms (*Cc, Ss, Vv*) and letters that look different (*Aa, Ee, Gg*). Students might come up with big letters, little letters, letters with tails, or letters they know and letters they don't know. As students sort encourage them to use the names of the letters and talk about their characteristics: "The letter *M* has zigzags."

Talk With: Exploring Real Coconuts

Opening a coconut takes some work but most children will never have the experience anywhere else so give it a try. For this language experience you will need a fresh coconut, a hammer and nail, several plastic shopping bags, a screwdriver, and a grater. Pass around the coconut, shake it, and encourage children to describe it—*round, hard, rough, hairy,* and so on. It is especially important for English learners that they be encouraged to talk as much as possible using new words that come up. Help them compose a short sentence like "The coconut is . . ." (The word for *coconut* in Spanish and French is very similar—*coco.*) Ask children for ideas about what might be inside and how you might get it open.

Using the nail or other sharp instrument hammer or punch a hole through two of the three eyes and drain out the coconut milk. It should be clear and sweet smelling. Then put the coconut inside a plastic bag inside another bag and bash it against a hard surface (such as a sidewalk or steps) several times to break the coconut into pieces. You can also crack it with a hammer. Pry out chunks of the coconut meat with a screwdriver or chisel and then wash it off and pass out small pieces to the students to examine and taste. It is not necessary to remove the brown skin of the meat. Again ask them to describe it— *white, creamy, chewy, moist,* and so on. Demonstrate how to shred the coconut using the grater and ask children to name foods they have eaten containing coconut. You could break open the coconut at home and bring in the pieces to show and taste while bringing in a whole coconut as well.

Write With

After the previous language experience, gather a group of children and ask them to talk about it. Give them time to review what was said about the coconut and what was done with it. Explain that you would like to write down some of their ideas and record their dictations on a chart. For children in the emergent stage it is helpful to start each sentence with their name and limit the number to no more than five sentences. You can start off with the topic sentence and then record students' ideas. It might look something like this:

> Mr. Edwards brought a coconut to school.
>
> Marley said, "It was brown and fuzzy."
>
> Leon said, "We had to break it open."
>
> Roberto said, "It was white inside."
>
> Teresa said, "I want my Mom to get a coconut."

Say each word slowly as you write and select some words to model phoneme segmentation and letter–sound matching. For example, "The next word is *fuzzy.* Let's say it slowly—/ffffuuzzzz-eee/. What sound does it start with? /fffffffuzzy/? Yes, /f/. What letter do we need to write that sound? Yes, *f.* Who can point to the letter *f* on our chart? We need a lowercase *f* in this word and this is how I will make it. What sound comes next? /fuuuuuzee/. I hear /uh/ in that word and I need to use the letter *u.* Who can find that letter on the chart? What letter comes next? /fuzzzzzzzz-e/? What letter do we need for the /z/ sound?"

You can be selective, not needing to model like this with every word. Pick words in which the correspondences are straightforward like *we, had,* or *it.* Also model how to find names (*Marley, Leon*), color words (*brown, white*), and other classifications on charts or word walls in the classroom. Ask students to tell you the letters in the words as you write them down.

For English learners you might simplify the language by creating a patterned text in which students supply words that describe the coconut in a frame sentence: "The coconut was _____" (*round, brown, hard, good to eat, sweet,* etc.). Repeat the same patterned sentence with variations or even with two supplied words, such as "*Rosa* said, the coconut was *brown.*"

ALPHABET TRACKING

We have provided an alphabet tracking strip on page 95 that can be used in a variety of ways. You can use it as is, or cut it apart and glue it together to create one long strip. Make one for children to take home, to keep at their seats, or to use in small groups. Alphabet strips should be posted in the writing center and used as a reference during writing activities. While large-scale alphabet charts may be posted for reference, young children will benefit more from having a small alphabet strip within easy reach that they can touch and study up close.

The strip can be used for the following activities, among many others:

1. For tracking practice, provide all students with a strip and ask them to touch the letters as they recite or sing the alphabet song. Do this over and over to reinforce letter recognition, sequence, left-to-right orientation, and return sweep. You should periodically try saying the letters backwards by starting at *Z*.

2. Have children find and touch letters on their strip as you or another child calls them aloud. For example: "Find and touch the letter *p*. Find the letter at the beginning of Jenny's name. Find the letter you need to spell the first sound in *turtle*." If you feature children's names as described in *Words Their Way* under *One Child's Name,* have children find all the letters in the name of the featured child.

3. You can use the alphabet strip as a record of the letters that students know by coloring in the letter boxes as they are mastered.

4. Give students a second strip and ask them to cut apart the letters. (Enlarge the strip to maximum size before making copies.) Then ask the students to put the letters back in order (with or without a second strip as a reference, depending on the student's skill level). These can be glued down.

5. Cut apart the alphabet strip to serve as the letter headers for the Alphabet Scrapbook described above.

ALPHABET SQUARES FOR SEQUENCING AND MATCHING

See pages 96 and 97 for letter cards that can be used in various games and matching activities. Print copies of these letter cards (enlarge as much as possible) onto card stock, cut apart, and use them as letter props. The simplest activities will involve matching letters that are exactly the same. For example, students can match *M–M, P–P, S–S,* and so on.

When students easily match capital to capital letters, work on matching lowercase to lowercase letters, and finally to matching the uppercase versions of letters to their lowercase partners. Again, work with a limited set when the activity is first introduced, and add more letter pieces if students need to be challenged. If students know most letters, mix in known and unknown letters for targeted practice.

Sequencing letters is a good activity. Provide letter cards, letter tiles, molded letters, or magnetic letters, and ask students to put the letters in order. Observe to see how readily they do this. Do they recite the alphabet before adding the next letter? If so they are getting lots of practice, but over time they should be able to do it more automatically. Provide a letter strip only if it is needed.

Of course these letters can also be used as game pieces for Concentration or Lotto. When playing concentration or memory students can match capitals to capitals, lowercase to lowercase, and capitals to lowercase. This is a good way to work on targeted letters. Limit the number to ten pairs or less and mix in both known letters and letters that need practice.

LETTER LOTTO

Students enjoy playing Lotto or Bingo with their letters. A 16-square blackline is included on page 98 as a template. Make boards by either writing letters in the squares or by pasting letters from the alphabet squares on pages 96 or 97. The letters can be cut apart for the draw pile. Have students draw from the pile, call out the letter, and place a bingo marker on the matching letter. The winner is the first to get four in a row. Later, students can play a similar game with beginning sounds; for example, see Initial Sound Bingo in *Words Their Way* among other beginning activities in the letter name–alphabetic stage.

FONT SORTS

Students in the emergent stage who are learning their letters need to learn both uppercase and lowercase forms, which can take some time. While the capital and lowercase forms of some letters vary only in size (such as *S* and *s*), others look very different (such as *A* and *a*). Lowercase letters are sometimes called "little" letters, but lowercase *l* is really no smaller than capital *I*, so that term is somewhat ambiguous. We prefer to use the term "capital" for the uppercase letters and "lowercase" for the others.

Young readers must learn to recognize letters despite the variation in letter styles that abound in the world of print. Obvious examples include the lowercase *g* and *a* found in most printed material that look very different from the manuscript forms teachers are likely to model in their writing or have on alphabet charts in the classroom. Less obvious, but still potentially confusing, are serifs, curly tails, and variations in line width. For this reason we feel it is helpful to draw students' attention to these differences and even to celebrate the rich variety through font sorts and font searches.

We have included a set of blackline masters on pages 99–107 that have five different font styles for each capital and lowercase letter. We suggest that you select from these as you study the letters both for letter recognition and letter–sound connections. For example, if you are focusing on the letters *B* and *M*, make a copy of the *B* and *M* font sorts and create a center activity or develop a handout for students to cut apart and sort for seatwork. Enlarge these as much as 50 percent for modeling or for use in centers. You may also want to paste them on squares of a heavier paper such as construction paper or card stock and laminate them. Be sure to use the same color for all the cards, or a random assortment of colors so that color does not offer a clue for sorting. There are several font sorts on the *Words Their Way* CD-ROM ready to print out and use: A and B; D, G, and E; and M, N, and H.

Demonstrate the Font Sorts

When font sorts are first introduced they should be modeled by the teacher. Begin by laying out the letter cards (both capital and lowercase) for one letter so that children can see them all. Use as a header the letter cards you think your students are most likely to recognize. (We used Century Gothic for the first column as it seems closest to the manuscript used in primary classrooms.) Explain, "Here is capital *A* and here is lowercase *a*." Select another letter card and think aloud as you explain. "Hmmm, this looks a little different because it has fat lines (or curly lines, slants, etc.) but it is still a capital *A*, so I am going to put it under the other capital *A*." Continue like this for one or two more cards and then invite your students to choose a card, talk about it, and sort it under either the capital or the lowercase header. See if they can articulate some of the differences using their own words.

Sort, Check, and Reflect

Mix up all the letters except the headers and have the children sort them again under your supervision. Talk about how letters come in both capital and lowercase forms and how we use capitals for the first letter in names. Look around the classroom for more examples and ask students to find and point to specific letters in the charts they are using for shared reading.

Extend

On another day add a second set of letters so that you have two capital and two lowercase letters to compare. Start with obvious contrasts like *A* and *B*, but if students know most of the letters try contrasting the ones that they often confuse such as *B* and *D* or *P* and *Q*. When comparing the lowercase forms of those letters draw a line along the bottom of the letter cards so that students can orient them correctly. Eventually you can contrast up to four letters at a time.

Encourage children to go on letter hunts at home or at school, looking through newspapers, magazines, advertisements, and so on, to find even more examples of letter styles. Children can add these to their own Alphabet Scrapbooks, or they can put them on a sheet of construction paper and post them in the classroom. Later these sheets can become pages and be made into a big book of letters. Pictures of things that begin with the letter's sound can also be added.

Letters _____ Reads			
A a		N n	
B b		O o	
C c		P p	
D d		Q q	
E e		R r	
F f		S s	
G g		T t	
H h		U u	
I i		V v	
J j		W w	
K k		X x	
L l		Y y	
M m		Z z	

Chicka Chicka Boom Boom

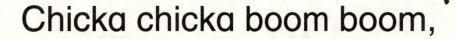

Chicka chicka boom boom,

Will there be enough room?

Here comes ___ up the coconut tree.

a b c d e f g h i j k l m

n o p q r s t u v w x y z

Reprinted with the permission of Simon and Schuster Books for Young Readers, an imprint of Simon & Schuster Children's Publishing Division, from Chicka Chicka Boom Boom by Bill Martin Jr. and John Archambault. Text copyright © 1989 Bill Martin Jr. and John Archambault.

93

	Aa	Bb
Cc	Dd	Ee
Gg	Ii	Jj
Kk	Pp	Qq
Tt	Uu	Vv
Ww	Yy	Zz

Alphabet Tracking Strip

Aa Bb Cc Dd Ee Ff Gg Hh

Ii Jj Kk Ll Mm Nn Oo Pp Qq

Rr Ss Tt Uu Vv Ww Xx Yy Zz

Alphabet Squares (Capitals)

A	B	C	D	E
F	G	H	I	J
K	L	M	N	O
P	Q	R	S	T
U	V	W	X	Y
Z				

Alphabet Squares (Lowercase)

a	b	c	d	e
f	g	h	i	j
k	l	m	n	o
p	q	r	s	t
u	v	w	x	y
z				

SORT 14   Letter Lotto Board

a	*a*	a	a	ᵃ
A	*A*	A	A	A
b	*b*	b	b	b
B	*B*	B	B	B
C	*C*	c	C	c
C	*C*	C	C	C

d	d	d	d	d
D	D	D	D	D
e	e	e	e	e
E	E	E	E	E
f	f	f	f	f
F	F	F	F	F

g	*g*	g	**g**	g
G	*G*	G	**G**	G
h	*h*	h	**h**	h
H	*H*	H	**H**	H
i	*i*	i	**i**	i
l	*I*	I	**l**	I

j	*j*	j	**j**	j
J	*J*	J	**J**	J
k	**k**	k	**k**	k
K	**K**	K	**K**	K
l	**l**	l	**l**	l
L	**L**	L	**L**	L

m	*m*	m	**m**	m
M	*M*	M	**M**	M
n	*n*	n	**n**	n
N	*N*	N	**N**	N
O	*O*	O	**O**	O
O	*O*	O	**O**	O

p	p	p	p	p
P	P	P	P	P
q	q	q	q	q
Q	Q	Q	Q	Q
r	r	r	r	r
R	R	R	R	R

S	*S*	S	**S**	S
S	*S*	S	**S**	S
t	*t*	t	**t**	t
T	*T*	T	**T**	T
U	*u*	u	**u**	u
U	*u*	U	**U**	U

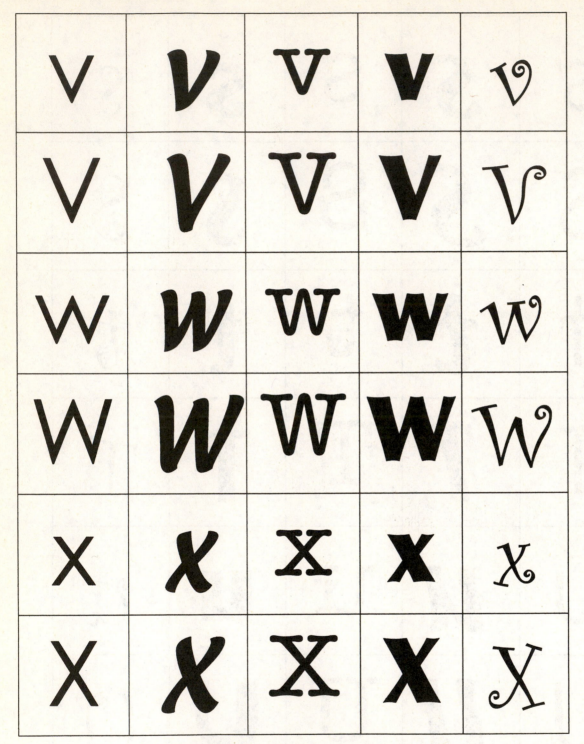

Y	y	y	y	y
Y	Y	Y	Y	y
Z	z	z	z	z
Z	Z	Z	Z	z

Chapter 5   Beginning Consonant Sounds

NOTES FOR THE TEACHER

In this chapter we provide you with resources for teaching beginning consonant sounds. We describe two units featuring the folk tale of the gingerbread man and the nursery rhyme *Hey Diddle Diddle,* describing in detail how to introduce the sound sorts and providing prepared picture sorts. There are 15 additional reading selections for which we suggest sorting contrasts and other follow-up activities. For these and other texts you like to use with your students we provide a collection of *letter pages* that feature pictures for a single consonant. Children cannot sort unless they have two or more sounds to contrast, but we have created these one-sound pages to make it easier to sequence and group sounds to match any core reading program. With these resources we hope that you will integrate phonics with the variety of reading materials available in your classrooms (big books, poems, songs, etc.), differentiating instruction as needed.

Targeted Learners

All students in the emergent stage should participate in these activities, but some students will be able to handle a faster pace with more categories. If students are struggling to sort accurately, spend a bit more time on two sounds, and then add a third and a fourth. Across the emergent stage, developmental level determines pacing.

- Early emergent learners may know few if any letter names and are unable to match pictures that begin with the same phoneme as in the Beginning Sound: Alliteration assessment in Chapter 1. While preschool teachers might focus just on learning the alphabet, in kindergarten students need to learn to listen for sounds at the beginnings of words at the same time as they learn the names of letters. They should sort pictures that offer a clear contrast (such as *m* and *s*), focusing on just two letter–sound correspondences at a time and engaging in lots of practice before moving on to new correspondences. One way to get started listening for beginning sounds is to personalize it by using students' names. If the student's name is Matt, for example, help him to find pictures that start with *M* (*mouse, milk*) and compare with pictures that do not (*sun, rain*).
- Middle emergent learners will know many letter names and may begin these activities with some awareness of letter–sound correspondences. They should systematically work with all the initial consonants and can sort two to four sounds at a time, starting with clear contrasts.
- Late emergent spellers know most letters of the alphabet and will score 50 percent or more on the Assessment of Beginning Consonant Sounds described in Chapter 1. On the spelling inventory or in their writing, they will represent some beginning sounds. They will benefit from a fast-paced overview of consonants with repeated practice that increases the accuracy and speed of their sorting. They can sort less obvious contrasts (like *b* and *p*) and learn the less frequent sounds (like *y* and *w*).

Teaching Tips

At the emergent level it is particularly important to introduce sounds and letters in meaningful contexts so that students can see the purpose for learning those confusing little black marks and those abstract sounds. For this reason we provide reading selections to use as a starting point for the study of letter–sound correspondences and we also refer you back to earlier selections. We encourage you to look through your own collections of favorite poems, songs, jingles, chart stories, big books, and so on for texts that feature particular letters. *Mrs. Wishy Washy,* a favorite book from the Wright Group Story Box (by Joy Cowley), is a natural link with the letter *w. Jump, Frog, Jump!* (by Robert Kalen) features the word *jump* throughout and therefore links to the letter *j.* Themes and topics of study can also become the starting point for word study. For example, in February ask students to dictate sentences about valentines and then introduce or review the sound of the letter *v.*

On pages 112–113 you will find a chart of all the selections in this book and the words that begin with salient beginning consonant sounds. Use this to find a selection to introduce sounds as well as selections that can be used for word hunts or follow-up reading. Concrete words like *fish* and *hands* can become the key words in a picture sort while more abstract words like *will* and *want* are good words to find in a word hunt. Looking through this chart you will see that some words repeat across three or more selections (i.e. *hands, man, rain, two*). This repetition will support English learners' acquisition of new vocabulary and all children's acquisition of sight words, making them good candidates for students' word banks. High frequency words like *the, is, was, to, and, on, it,* and *in* will also occur across selections and are good candidates for both word banks and word walls.

For the teacher demonstration sorts make a copy of the pictures you need, enlarging them as much as possible to use in a pocket chart or on a table or rug. Additional pictures can be found in the Appendix of *Words Their Way.* You may want to create a master set of pictures that you color and laminate to reuse over and over. To create handouts that students will cut apart to sort, make a copy of the pictures you need (using the letter pages or pictures from *Words Their Way*) and paste them randomly on the templates in the Appendix. In this way you can control the sequence. The *Words Their Way* CD-ROM has prepared sets of initial sounds sorts that contrast three sounds at a time as well as prepared game boards. This variety of resources enables you to take many different paths for the study of initial sounds, depending on your students' needs and the sequence preferred.

Directions for leading the sorting activity are described in detail for the first two selections in this chapter using the four basic steps in a small-group word study activity: Demonstrate, Sort and Check, Reflect, and Extend. Chapter 4 of *Words Their Way* provides additional background information about consonants and guidelines for sorting. You will find games in the activities section of that chapter, such as Alphabet Spin for Sounds and Follow-the-Path, that extend children's learning as they continue to practice in engaging ways. The Sound Board for Beginning Consonants and Digraphs in the Appendix of *Words Their Way* is a reference tool to study beginning sounds. Students should have a copy of a Sound Board in their personal readers and writing books. They might color in the sounds as they are studied using a light-colored crayon or marker.

Word Study with English Language Learners

It is very likely that at least some of the sounds in an English learner's home language differ from the sounds in English. In most cases English has more sounds than other languages that students need to perceive and learn to pronounce and spell. Some of the sound properties of consonants are highlighted in Table 5.1 to provide a sense of the types of confusions or substitutions that are common for English learners. For example, students with Spanish-language backgrounds may respond that *goat* and *car* sound alike at the beginning. When students think of words that sound the same as other words, they may include words that sound the same in their dialect or language, but not yours. For example, a student may say *sew* for *show* and consider it to be an example of an *s* word. Accept students' contributions as accurate given their dialect. Pointing out the difference at that time may be useful, and these contrasts are made later when students have mastery of the basic contrasts.

If you have Spanish-speaking students with little knowledge of English you may want to use the five sorts on the *Words Their Way* CD-ROM that contrast consonants using Spanish words to match the pictures (*s m p, l c v, j d f, g r y, z ch ll*). Find out what students know in Spanish because this is likely to transfer to their learning in English. For example, Spanish-speaking students may know a good deal more about the Spanish vowels than students at the same stage know about English vowels because there are fewer vowel sounds in Spanish and they work in a more dependable fashion.

Children love to work in pairs, and this is especially helpful for English language learners. The English-speaking child can name the pictures that an English learner might not know. When students do not know the names of several pictures in a sort, have them focus on the pictures that they do know, and, if possible, find words and pictures that begin with the target sound in the student's oral language.

Teaching Consonant Blends and Digraphs, Final Consonant Sounds, and Vowels

Consonant blends, digraphs and short vowels need to be studied in some depth once students move into the letter name–alphabetic stage of spelling development. However,

TABLE 5.1 Predictable Consonant Confusions for ELs

B	The voiced B may sound more like the unvoiced P.	C	Hard C is often confused with hard G. Many languages do not have a hard C.
D	Often sounds like /th/ in Spanish (*dog* as *thog*).	F	Easily confused with V, especially in Arabic. In Japanese, it may be pronounced like h.
G	Hard G may be confused with K by speakers of Arabic, French, or Swahili.	H	Silent in Spanish. In Chinese it sounds more like /kh/ as in *loch*.
J	In Spanish represents the /h/ sound; J may also be pronounced like /ch/.	K	May be confused with /g/ by Spanish speakers, such as *gangaroo* for *kangaroo*.
L	May be confused with R; final L may be difficult.	M	May be dropped at the ends of words.
N	Speakers of Chinese may not pronounce this sound and confuse it with L. It may be dropped at the ends of words.	P	Easily confused with B because they are both formed with the lips and only differ in the vocal cords.
R	Rolled in Spanish; confused with L in Asian languages.	S	Difficult to perceive in final position.
T	May be substituted with /d/ by Spanish speakers and not pronounced at the ends of words.	V	May be confused with B in Spanish and Korean. It does not exist in many languages and may be substituted with /f/.
W	Spanish speakers may pronounce this with more of a /gw/ sound, saying *gwen* for *when*.	Y	This sound may be more like /ch/ in Spanish, as in *chew* for *you*.
Z	May be pronounced like the /s/ sound in Spanish and not voiced.			

Title	Page	B	hard C	D	F	hard G	H	J	K	L
Animals	48	birds			fly fish			jump		
Chicka Chicka Boom Boom	93	boom be	comes coconut				here			
Circles	46	board								
Five Little Ducks	185	but back	came	ducks day	five far		hills			little
Fuzzy Wuzzy	145	bear			fuzzy		had hair he			
Gingerbread Man	126		can can't catch		fast					
Good Morning to You	137			dear		good				
Happy Birthday	198	birthday		dear			happy			
Hey Diddle Diddle	130		cat cow	diddle dog dish	fiddle fun			jumped		little laughed
Hickory Dickory Dock	139			dickory dock down						
Hop a Little, Jump a Little	138	bend bed					hop head	jump		little
Humpty Dumpty	23		couldn't	Dumpty	fall		Humpty had horses		king's	
Jack and Jill	143		came	down	fetch fell		hill	Jack Jill		
Jump Rope	190							jump just		
Lollipops	141					good				lollipop lick
My Fruit	42	banana bowl	cut							
Oh, A-Hunting We Will Go	68	box	catch		fox	go	him			let
Old Mister Rabbit	135		cabbage			got garden	habit	jumping		
On the Bed	192	bed		dog						
One, Two, Buckle My Shoe	195	buckle big		door	four five fat		hen			lay
Open and Close	72					go	hands here			
Pat a Cake, Pat a Cake	134	bake baker baby	cake can	dot	fast					
Peas Porridge Hot	188		cold	days			hot			
Rags	199			dog			have his he			
Rain	140		come	day		go				little
Rain on the Green Grass	180	but					housetop			
Raining	183	bed bumped	couldn't			get	he his head			
Row Your Boat	194	boat but		down						life
Socks, Shoes, Caps, and Gloves	50		cap		feet		head hands			
Soft Kitty	142	ball			fur		happy		kitty	little
Teddy Bear, Teddy Bear	136	bear				goodnight				lights
This Is the Way	52						hands			
Valentines	146									love
Yo-Yo	147		can			go	have			
Zoo	201		can come			go			kangaroo	let's like

M	N	P	R	S	T	V	W	Y	Z
monkeys				swim			water		
			room				will		
make		paper							
mother				said			went		
	no						Wuzzy was wasn't		
me man			run					you	
morning					to			you	
					to			you	
moon			ran	see such	to		with		
mouse			ran						
	nod		run		two tap			yawn	
men		put		sat	together		wall		
		pail			tumbling to		went water		
miss			rope				will watch		
my		put peel					wash		
							we we'll will		
mister mighty			rabbit					you've	
my mama		papa		sits sister					
my	nine	pick		seven six	two ten				
mouths							we		
man mark me		pat put					with	you	
	nine	peas porridge pot							
much	name		Rags	so sags	tummy tail		wig wags walks		zig-zag
			rain	some			wants		
me	not		rain						
man morning		pouring	raining		to		went		
merrily			row					your	
		put		socks	toes				
		purr		soft			warm		
				say	Teddy touch turn				
morning				so			way we wash		
			red	says		valentines		you	
	no				toe			yo-yo you yellow	
					to too		we	you	zoo zebra

113

all these features should be introduced to some extent as you write with children in activities such as Morning Message or when you take dictations. Model how to segment all the phonemes (including blends, digraphs, and vowels) and match them to letters. When students write, encourage them to listen for other sounds in the words and represent them as best they can. By modeling and encouraging you can foreshadow the formal study of blends, digraphs, and vowels in the next stage.

You may study some final sounds once students have a firm understanding of several beginning consonant sounds. For example, you can emphasize the sound at the end of *bat* and observe how students recognize the final sounds of similar words. "Do *bat* and *car* sound alike at the end? Do *hat* and *goat* sound alike at the end?" Many students' oral language backgrounds and dialects do not include the same final sounds, and there will be deletions in spelling that are common to particular dialects in your area. Across several languages, we have found confusions around these final sounds: /-s/, /-t/, /-d/, /-p/, /-l/, /-r/, /-z/.

STANDARD ROUTINES FOR BEGINNING CONSONANT SORTS

Continue to integrate word study into your literacy instruction through the essential literacy activities discussed earlier: Read To, Read With, Talk With, and Word Study. The group sorting lesson should be followed up with repeated sorts as well as the other activities described below so that students have ample practice. Students should be able to sort accurately and quickly. As they become more proficient at these activities they can complete them independently. These and similar activities are discussed in Chapter 4 of *Words Their Way*.

1. *Read To: Literature Links.* Share literature in which sounds are embedded in rich oral language. Two types of literature are suggested:

   • Picture books that you read aloud can be used to introduce and reinforce beginning sounds and we recommend some titles in the Literature Connection box. For example, before or after enjoying *If You Give a Moose a Muffin* by Numeroff, you might draw attention to the words in the title that start with *M*. Do not ask

Literature Connection

Berenstein, S., & Berenstein, J. (1971). *The B book.* New York: Random House.

Calmenson, S. (2002). *The teeny tiny teacher.* New York: Scholastic.

Dr. Seuss. (1968). *The foot book.* New York: Random House.

Enderle, J. R. (1994). *Six snowy sheep.* Hanesdale, PA: Boyds Mills Press.

Kalen, R. (1989). *Jump, frog, jump!* New York: HarperTrophy.

MacDonald, S. (1994). *Sea shapes.* San Diego, CA: Gulliver Press, Harcourt Brace.

Massie, D. R. (2000). *The baby beebee bird.* New York: HarperCollins.

McLeod, E. (1975). *The bear's bicycle.* New York: Little Brown.

McPhail, D. (1996). *Pigs aplenty, pigs galore.* London: Puffin.

Numeroff, L. (1988). *If you give a moose a muffin.* New York: Scholastic.

O'Connor, J. (1997). *Benny's big bubble.* New York: Grosset.

Perkins, A. (1969). *Hand, hand, fingers, thumb.* New York: Random House.

students to listen for words that start with particular sounds as you read a book for the first time. Their attention will naturally be on the story as they listen to understand and find out what happens. Later you might go back and read a short piece of familiar text and ask them to listen for sounds.

- Selections of rhymes are provided in this chapter and throughout the book that feature one or more words that start with a targeted sound. Children enjoy reading them from memory and they support the development of concept of word in print, described in the next chapter. They can be used before sorting to introduce sounds or after sorting for a word hunt. Find more rhymes, jingles, and songs in the following suggested resources:

  Lipman, D. (1994). *We all go together: Creative activities for children to use with multicultural folksongs.* Phoenix, AZ: Oryx Press.
  http://bussongs.com (Words to hundreds of short and simple songs)
  http://curry.edschool.virginia.edu/go/wil/rimes_and_rhymes.htm   (Rhyme a Week)
  www.hubbardscupboard.org (Hubbards Cupboard—look under Mother Goose rhymes)

2. *Reread Selections.* Each student should get their own copy of the selections to put into personal readers that can be frequently revisited for rereading and word hunts. More information about personal readers can be found in the next chapter.

3. *Repeated Sorting.* The primary activity for students after a sort has been introduced in a group is to sort their pictures four to six times individually. After cutting up the pictures they can be stored in baggies or envelopes labeled with the child's name. Some teachers create sets of pictures that they use from year to year that are colored and laminated for students to use in centers or small groups. Other teachers create sorting folders such as described in *Words Their Way* for students to use. Chapter 3 of *Words Their Way* describes different options. Have students scribble over the back of the sort with a crayon before cutting as a way to identify their pictures.

4. *Word Hunts.* After studying sets of sounds, students should return to familiar reading selections where they look for words that begin with the targeted sound(s). They may go through their personal readers containing copies of familiar selections and dictations to find words. Alphabet books are also a good place to do a word hunt, but in this case students will find pictures for the targeted sound(s). If you are studying the letter *m*, have students find pages in various books that feature the letter to show the group. In this way students begin to use the rudimentary reference skill of finding things in alphabetical order. Expect some confusions to arise, however. Accept words with blends, as when a child says that *grass* begins with *g*. When a child finds words with digraphs (as in the *s* of *shoe*) or with soft *g* (as in *gingerbread*), be ready to explain that some words begin with the same letter but have a different sound. You may want to record the words students find in word hunts on a chart to reinforce the idea that the words are spelled with the same letter at the beginning. Students can underline or highlight words on their own copies of a selection and may even write some in their own Alphabet Scrapbooks.

5. *Alphabet Scrapbooks.* The Alphabet Scrapbooks described in the activities section of Chapter 4 in *Words Their Way* are a beginning dictionary that children create for themselves as they study letters and sounds. You may want to compile a class big book version using tagboard or chart paper. This may begin as a bulletin board activity. In individual scrapbooks, students can paste the bottom strip of the letter page as the heading of each page.

6. *Draw and Label/Cut and Paste.* Students are asked to think beyond the pictures given to them in the sort when they draw pictures of things that begin with the

sounds they have been studying. They should be encouraged to label the pictures, spelling as best they can. Help them say the word slowly to segment the phonemes and add letters beyond the first sound. Oral brainstorming is helpful before students are asked to draw things as they may have difficulty thinking of words. You might also suggest that they use an alphabet book as a reference for ideas. English learners may have difficulty thinking of words. Be ready to accept words in their native language that they draw for you.

One way to manage "cut and paste" and make it into a group activity is with Sound Buckets. Introduce a small bucket or box for each sound and label it with the beginning letter and key picture. Have children find pictures in magazines or catalogs, cut them out, and put them in the appropriate bucket. After a few days of collecting, students can join you in pasting them on a sheet of paper that can be posted on a bulletin board or added to the class Alphabet Scrapbook.

7. *Partner Sorts.* Students enjoy working together to sort, and they can help each other remember the names of the pictures. Letters or key pictures are laid down as headers. One student names the picture drawn from a pile while the other student indicates under which letter the picture goes. Children who are new to sorting will benefit from being paired up with a partner who understands the process but observe to be sure the less able partner is getting their turn.

8. *Alphabet Font Sorts.* As you work through the different letters in these sorts, add the appropriate font sorts from Chapter 4 as well. Children can look for capital and lowercase letters in newspapers and magazines and add them to Alphabet Scrapbooks.

9. *Assessment.* Ongoing assessment should take place as you observe how quickly and accurately students sort their pictures and how well they can represent the sounds they have studied when they write. After sorting the pictures repeatedly you can ask students to sort them into categories and then paste them down on paper and label them. This can serve as a summative assessment. Encourage students to spell as much of the word as they can, listening for all the sounds in the word. For example a student might spell *horse* as *HS.* This will give you information about whether students are hearing final consonants as well as initial. The assessments for beginning letter–sounds on pages 18, 19, and 20 can be used as a posttest when you have worked through all the sounds.

Letter Page Activities

Beginning consonant picture sorts are provided on pages 148 to 166.

1. Each page includes a collection of pictures for one beginning sound. These pictures must be combined with another letter page for a contrast. The first card on the first row is the letter in both capital and lowercase. The second card is the underlined key picture to use as a header for the sort. Pictures from two or more letter pages can be pasted onto a template in the Appendix to create a sort such as the *M* and *R* sort on page 127.

2. On the last two boxes of the third row, there is space for students to practice writing the letters. Point to the capital and lowercase letters saying, "Here are the capital and lowercase letters (*Mm*). Let me show you how to follow the arrows." Demonstrate at the table with students or on an overhead. Have students complete the letters on their own pages.

3. At the bottom of the page is a strip to introduce the sound. These strips can be posted in Alphabet Scrapbooks or stapled together with other letter page strips to create a little book. To the right of the picture is the letter in outline form followed by a line.

Some students may simply trace in the letter. Other students should be encouraged to write down "letters for all of the sounds you hear and feel when you say the name of this picture."

GINGERBREAD MAN (M & R)

Read To: Literature Link

The story of the gingerbread man is well known and available in many different versions. Begin by reading a version to your students (preferably one with the familiar refrain listed below). If you do not have a picture book version you can read it from an anthology of folk tales or tell it to the students. (You may be surprised at how enjoyable it is to be a storyteller!) Ask students to make predictions about what they think will happen, beginning with the cover of the book, in the manner of a directed listening thinking activity (DLTA). Invite children to join in the gingerbread man's refrain.

> Run, run as fast as you can.
> You can't catch me.
> I'm the gingerbread man.

Read With

Make a copy of the refrain from page 126 and enlarge it so it is easily read in a group. You might copy it onto a chart or sentence strips or display it using whatever technology you have available (overhead, active boards, etc). Remind the students that the gingerbread man laughed at the people and animals that chased him. Read the refrain as you point to the words and then ask the students to read along with you. Be explicit about how to point to *gingerbread.* Point to the word and say something like this: "Here is a long word. Let's see how many syllables are in *gingerbread* by clapping them: *gin-ger-bread.* That means we have to tap that word three times when we read it." Then give each child their own copy of the refrain and have them point with you. Students should add this selection to their personal readers and reread it often. (See ideas for the personal reader on page 168.)

Consonant Sort 16: *M & R*

1. *Prepare Materials.* Make copies of the sort for beginning sounds of *M* and *R* on page 127 to model. You may want to enlarge it 50 percent to make cards for sorting in a pocket chart. Make word cards for *man* and *run.*

2. *Context Connection.* Ask students to find two words in the refrain that start with the letter *M* (*man* and *me*). Show the word *man* on a card and point to the *M* at the beginning. Say, "*Man* starts with the letter *M.* Listen: *MMMMMan.* I hear /mmmm/ at the beginning of the word." Repeat with *run.* Find the word, hold it up on a card, and point to the first letter as you talk about how it begins with *R* and the /rrrrr/ sound. Put the pictures of man and run next to the word cards on a table top, in a pocket chart, or wherever students can see and manipulate the words and pictures.

3. *Model the Picture Sort.* Display the rest of the picture cards, naming each one with the student's help. If you have ELs, have them say the names of the pictures after you. (The initial *R* may be pronounced slightly differently by Spanish speakers and it may be confused with *L* by other ELs). Then explain that there are more words that begin with *M* and *R.* Pick out the picture of the monkey and say, "*MMMMMonkey. Man* and *monkey* begin with *M* so I will put this under the picture of the man."

Repeat with the ring. Model several more if necessary but begin to solicit student help by asking them to pick a picture, name it, and sort it under the letter it starts with. Offer support as needed to name the pictures, draw out the first sounds, and name the letters they go with.

4. *Resort, Reflect, and Check.* After sorting, name all the pictures under each letter, emphasizing the first sounds. Ask the students how all the words under each letter are the same ("They all begin with the sound for the letter *M*"). Take out all the pictures except for the man and run. Scramble them up and pass them out to the students to sort again. Let any mistakes go. After all the pictures have been sorted, demonstrate how to check them by naming all the pictures in each column and move any that are in the wrong place. Say something like this for errors: "Let's check the word *rope*, Listen—*rope man, rope run*. Does it start like *man* or *run*? We will put it over here under the *R*."

Extend: Day Two

1. *Read With.* Bring students together the next day and reread the refrain, both on the chart and on their own copies. Find the words *man* and *run*. Follow up with other personal reader activities as described in Chapter 6.

2. *Sort and Reflect.* Repeat the sort as a group for students who are new to sorting or for English learners who need more help naming the pictures. Then give students their own copy of the sort. Show them how to quickly scribble over the back using a different color for each student. (Warn them to work fast and only give them about 10 to 20 seconds to do this.) Then model how to cut the pictures apart by first cutting vertical columns and then snipping off each picture horizontally. Show them how to find the letters and the picture of man and run to use as headers; then ask them to sort the rest of the pictures the same way you sorted them as a group. Ask individual students to check by naming the pictures under a sound and then reflect by telling you how the pictures are alike. Give them a baggie or envelope to save their pictures to sort over several days.

Extend: Routines

1. *Resort.* Have students resort their pictures multiple times as suggested in the standard routines listed earlier in this chapter. If you use a pocket chart, make it available for sorting during the day. Students love to be the teacher and teach their classmates in just the same way you did. Students can sort their pictures again at their seats, in centers, or even at home.

2. *Word and Sound Hunt.* Show students how to do a word hunt by using other texts they have read with you or looking through their personal readers for familiar selections to find words that begin with *R* and *M*. Pass out a variety of alphabet books and ask students to find the *M* page and then the *R* page and share with others in the group what they found. If students have an Alphabet Scrapbook, develop the *R* and *M* pages by adding letters, words, drawings, and cut-out pictures.

3. *Draw and Label.* Brainstorm a list of things that begin with *M* and *R* and then ask students to do a draw and label activity. Fold a sheet of paper into four boxes, write *M* in two spaces and *R* in two spaces, and illustrate.

4. *Font Sort.* Students who are still learning the alphabet need more practice with letter identification and letter naming. On page 128 you will find a font sort created by pasting letters from pages 103 and 104 onto a template from the Appendix. Ask students to cut apart the letters and then sort them into four categories: *M, m, R,* and

r. Ask them to match capitals to lowercase by font styles. After sorting students can paste them onto a large sheet of paper folded into fourths.

Rhyme Sort 18

Ask students to find the rhyming words in the *Gingerbread Man* refrain (*man* and *can*). Follow up with the rhyme sort on page 129 that includes other words from the *–an* family (*fan, pan, van*) and contrast them with the *–at* family. You might save this sort to do after introducing *Hey Diddle Diddle*.

Read With and Talk With

Read other versions of *Gingerbread Man* and talk about the similarities and differences. Talk about how artists illustrate it differently and how some say *boy* while others say *man*. In some versions the runaway is a pancake, a journey cake, or a tortilla. We list some titles in the Literature Connection box but you will find many more when you begin looking.

Write With and Write Independently

Invite children to complete the frame sentence: "I ran away from a _____." Students can also be encouraged to pick their favorite part of the story to illustrate. They can then be encouraged to label it or write a sentence about it, spelling as best they can.

HEY DIDDLE DIDDLE (C & D)

Notes for the Teacher

The letter *c* is first introduced as the hard sound /k/, so expect some confusion as children hunt for words that begin with *c*. You can explain that students are correct when they want to say that the letter *c* makes an /s/ sound. You can create a separate category for such pictures: "I put the word *circle* over here, because, yes, it has the letter *c* at the beginning, but it has an /sss/ sound like the word *sun*." When asked to think of words that begin with *c*, students may think of words that begin with the letter *k*. You can tell them about words that sound the same but begin with a different letter. For example, "Kate's name begins with a *k*, and it sounds the same as the beginning of *cake*, which begins with a *c*."

Literature Connection

Aylesworth, J. (1998). *The gingerbread man.* New York: Scholastic.

Egielski, R. (2000). *The gingerbread boy.* New York: HarperTrophy.

Galdone, P. (1983). *The gingerbread boy.* New York: Clarion.

Kimmell, E. A. (2000). *The runaway tortilla.* New York: Winslow Press

Mackinnon, M., Sims, L., & Provantini, S. (2006). *The runaway pancake.* Eveleth, MN: Usborne Books.

Schmidt, K. (1985). *The gingerbread man.* New York: Scholastic.

Sawyer, R., & McCloskey, R. (1953). *Journey Cake, Ho!* Delron, NJ: Weekly Reader Children's Book Club.

Read With

The nursery rhyme on page 130 is a favorite. Enlarge the pictures on page 131 and use them to orally introduce children to *Hey Diddle Diddle*. Hold up a picture for each line and then have students repeat each line in an echo fashion. Use the pictures to teach vocabulary to your English learners by pointing to the cat, cow, and moon and other objects named in the poem. Create an enlarged copy of the text so all the students in your group can see the print. Point to the words as you read each line and invite children to point. Give each student a copy of the rhyme to practice pointing.

Hey Diddle Diddle

Hey diddle diddle, the cat and the fiddle.
The cow jumped over the moon.
The little dog laughed to see such fun
And the dish ran away with the spoon.

Create sentence strips for each line of the poem (page 131) and use them to rebuild the poem. Give children a second copy of the poem that they can cut apart and rebuild it the same way, placing each line beside a picture. Save the pieces to repeat on a second or third day and then supply paper so that students can paste it down.

Consonant Sort 19: *C & D*

1. *Introduce the Sort.* Make a copy of the sort on page 132 with pictures for beginning consonants *C* and *D*. Prepare word cards for *cat, cow, dog, duck.* Hold up the letter *C* and ask students to find words in the text that start with *c* (*cat, cow*). Put the word and picture of the cat and the cow under *C* and say. "Listen to the first sound in *cat* and *cow*. They begin with the letter *C*" (point to the letter at the beginning of each word as it is named). Repeat with *D, dog,* and *dish.* Display and name the rest of the pictures and then hold up another picture and say, "Listen to the first sound in this word. Will I put it with *cat* and *cow* under *C*, or with *dog* and *dish* under *D*?" Sort all the pictures, eliciting student help, and then place them in columns while emphasizing the first sound.

2. *Sort, Check, and Reflect.* Prepare a copy of the sort for the children to cut apart and sort. Ask individual children to name the pictures under each letter and to tell you how they are alike. Store the pieces to sort again on another day and use the follow-up activities from page 118.

Extend

See Extend: Routines on pages 118 and 119. Include these as well.

1. *Word Hunt.* Review the refrain from *The Gingerbread Man* to look for words that start with *C* (*can* and *catch*).

2. *Compare Four Sounds.* Combine all the pictures for *M, R, C,* and *D* and sort under the key words and letters.

3. *Font Sort.* Use the font sort on page 128 to compare *Mm* and *Rr. C* is not included because the capital and lowercase forms are the same, but you could add if desired.

4. *Sight Words and Word Banks.* There are a number of high-frequency words in this poem that are good choices to teach as sight words to students in the middle to late emergent stage: *the, cat, and, little, dog, to, see, ran,* or *with.* Select two or three to focus on. Students may self-select more concrete words for their word bank such as *moon* or *cow.* See *Words Their Way* and Chapter 6 to read more about word banks.

Concept Sort 20: Real and Make Believe

Make a copy of the concept sort for real and make believe on page 133 and enlarge it for modeling. Explain that nursery rhymes often have make believe characters who do things real animals can't do. Show the picture of the cat and the fiddle. Ask children if cats really play fiddles (or violins). Put the header "make believe" in a pocket chart or lay it on a table and put the cat and the fiddle under it. Point to and read the words "make believe." Then show the picture of the real cat sleeping. Ask the children if this is make believe or real and why—cats really do sleep. Put it under the heading "real" and point to the word. Continue with the other pictures.

Talk With and Write With: Real and Make Believe

Use the pictures from the concept sort to stimulate a discussion and brainstorming session with the children about real and make believe. Ask the students for ideas about what real cats do and what make believe cats might do. Repeat this with the other animals. If you have English learners help them to name the animals and invite the children to act out ideas as well as describe them. For example as you say, "Real cats climb trees," everyone can dramatize it. Then select two sentences to record on a chart. First, write up the title "Real and Make Believe," Ask students for ideas about things real animals do and then something the same animal might do as make believe. Record children's ideas such as the ones below. As you write, say each word slowly and write the letter for the sound you make. Reread each sentence after you write it, pointing to each word.

> Real cats play with balls.
> Make believe cats drive cars.

Read To

Read additional rhymes from a collection of nursery rhymes, especially those that feature make believe characters and events. Explain that the collections of nursery rhymes are often called "Mother Goose Nursery Rhymes" and read the title of several different collections. Then read aloud other nursery rhymes, looking through the illustrations and helping the children identify real and make believe situations. You could add to your real and make believe concept sort by making photocopies of illustrations or downloading pictures from online resources. Make the real and make believe sort available for students to do in a center.

THE REMAINING SELECTIONS

The remaining selections in this chapter are not developed as fully as the first two. Use the chart on pages 112 and 113 to help you make decisions about which selections to choose for the sounds you want to introduce or reinforce. Continue with Read To, Read With, Talk With, Write With, and Word Study activities as you use these to introduce beginning consonant sounds or for word hunts. See the standard routines described earlier in this chapter for ideas about ways to enhance students' mastery of beginning letter–sound correspondences.

Pat a Cake, Pat a Cake

This selection (see page 134) emphasizes the hard *c* sound with *cake* and *can*. Use it to introduce *b* (*baby, bake, baker*), and revisit *m* (*man, mark, me*). It is also a good place to review a number of other letters and sounds.

Children enjoy pantomiming these actions. They pat the dough and enjoy substituting their own letters for the *B*. One student opens the door to the pretend oven while the other extends arms to place the tray inside. Students substitute the first letter of their partner's name for *B*, and their partner's name for *baby*: "*Mark it with a P . . . for Pedro and me.*"

Pat a Cake, Pat a Cake

Pat a cake, pat a cake, baker's man!
Bake me a cake as fast as you can,
Pat it, and dot it, and mark it with a B,
And put it in the oven
For baby and me.

Old Mister Rabbit

This is a traditional song or chant (see page 135) that Doug Lipman describes in *We All Go Together*. The two ending lines are ideal for sentence frames and fill-ins. He suggests changing the food, and then changing where the rabbit jumps, for example, "Of jumping in my kitchen, And eating our spaghetti." Use this rhyme to introduce *y* (*you're*), *h* (*habit*), *g* (*garden*), and perhaps *j* (*jumping*). *G* and *J* are a hard contrast but one that students in the late emergent stage should be ready for. Revisit it for *m* (*mister, mighty*) and *c* (*cabbage*).

Old Mister Rabbit

Old Mister Rabbit,
You've got a mighty habit,
Of jumping in my garden
And eating all my cabbage.

Teddy Bear, Teddy Bear

This is a jump rope rhyme (see page 136) that young students like to act out. Use it to introduce *t* (*teddy, turn, touch*) and *l* (*lights*), and revisit *b* (*bear*), *s* (*say*), and *g* (*goodnight*).

Teddy Bear, Teddy Bear

Teddy Bear, Teddy Bear, turn around.
Teddy Bear, Teddy Bear, touch the ground.
Teddy Bear, Teddy Bear, turn out the lights.
Teddy Bear, Teddy Bear, say goodnight!

Good Morning to You

Sing this selection (see page 137) to the tune of *Happy Birthday*. This is a cheerful song to sing as you come together in the morning, substituting student names. Use it to revisit *g* (*good*), *m* (*morning*), and *y* (*you*).

Good Morning to You

Good morning to you
Good morning to you
Good morning dear _____ (someone's name),
Good morning to you.

Hop a Little, Jump a Little

The two-syllable word "little" calls for careful tracking when students reread this piece (see page 138). Use it to introduce *n* (*nod*). Revisit *h* (*hop, head*), *b* (*bed, bend*), *t* (*two, tap*), *y* (*yawn, your*), and *l* (*little*).

Hop a Little, Jump a Little

Hop a little, jump a little,
One, two, three;
Run a little, skip a little,
Tap one knee;
Bend a little, stretch a little,
Nod your head;
Yawn a little, sleep a little,
In your bed.

Hickory Dickory Dock

Many children will know this familiar rhyme (see page 139). Recite it together before you show the printed form. Talk about grandfather clocks and show the picture (perhaps from a nursery rhyme collection) so children will understand how a mouse might run up and down a clock. Use it to revisit *m* (*mouse*), *d* (*dickory, dock, down*), or *r* (*ran*).

Hickory Dickory Dock

Hickory dickory dock,
The mouse ran up the clock!
The clock struck one.
The mouse ran down.
Hickory dickory dock.

Rain

Use this rhyme (see page 140) to introduce *s* (*some*) or *w* (*wants*). Revisit it for *r* (*rain, Rosie*), *c* (*come*), *d* (*day*), and *g* (*go*). Replace the name *Rosie* with the names of children in your class.

Rain

Rain, rain, go away,
Come again some other day.
Little Rosie wants to play.

Lollipops

This poem (see page 141) is ideal for syllabication and for finding the three *l*s inside *Lollipops*. Have students pretend to lick the lollipop in cadence with "*Lick, lick, lick.*" Use this rhyme to revisit *l* (*lick, lollipop*) and *g* (*good*). Have children illustrate this one.

Lollipops

Lollipops, lollipops,
Lick, lick, lick.
Lollipops, lollipops,
Good on the stick.

Soft Kitty

K is a surprisingly rare letter but this poem can be used to focus on it (see page 142).

> **Soft Kitty**
>
> Soft kitty, warm kitty,
> Little ball of fur.
> Sleepy kitty, happy kitty,
> Purr, purr, purrrrrrrr.

Jack and Jill

Students move their fingers walking up the hill and tumbling down as they recite the rhyme (see page 143). Use this rhyme to introduce *p* (*pail*), *f* (*fell, fetch*), and *w* (*went, water*). Revisit for *j* (*Jack, Jill*), *h* (*hill*), *d* (*down*), and *c* (*came*). A concept sort can be created of things that you would find outside (on the hill) and things you would find inside (where Jack is laid up after his accident). Use the sentence strips to cut apart and rebuild the rhyme as described for *Hey Diddle Diddle*.

> **Jack and Jill**
>
> Jack and Jill went up the hill
> To fetch a pail of water.
> Jack fell down
> And broke his crown.
> And Jill came tumbling after.

Fuzzy Wuzzy

Find the *z*s in this poem (see page 145). Reciting this favorite tickles as the *z*s vibrate. Use this rhyme to introduce *z* (in *fuzzy* and *wuzzy*) and revisit *b* (*bear*), *h* (*hair, had, he*), and *w* (*wuzzy, was*).

> **Fuzzy Wuzzy**
>
> Fuzzy Wuzzy
> was a bear,
> Fuzzy Wuzzy
> had no hair,
> Fuzzy Wuzzy
> wasn't really fuzzy,
> Was he?

Valentines

V is a rare letter but is nicely featured as a beginning consonant in this jingle (see page 146).

> **Valentines**
>
> Valentines red
> Valentines blue
> This valentine says
> "I love you."

Yo-Yo

Here is a poem (see page 147) we have created especially for *y*. Not all children will be familiar with a yo-yo so bring one in to demonstrate how it works and then let them try it.

> I have a yellow yo-yo
> And it can really go, go
> You can try it.
> Oh, no!
> It wrapped around my toe, toe.

Name_____ Date _____ Number _____

Gingerbread Man

Run, run as fast as you can.

You can't catch me.

I'm the gingerbread man.

m	*m*	m	m	m
M	**M**	M	**M**	M
r	**r**	r	r	r
R	**R**	R	**R**	R

SORT 18   Rhyming Sort

can	cat	

Name_____ Date _____ Number _____

Hey Diddle Diddle

Hey diddle diddle

The cat and the fiddle

The cow jumped

over the moon.

The little dog laughed

to see such fun.

And the dish ran away

with the spoon.

Sentence Strips for *Hey Diddle Diddle*

Hey Diddle Diddle

Hey diddle diddle, the cat and the fiddle

The cow jumped over the moon.

The little dog laughed to see such fun.

And the dish ran away with the spoon.

Concept Sort for Real and Make Believe

Name_____   Date/Story Number_____

Pat a Cake, Pat a Cake

Pat a cake, pat a cake, baker's man,

Bake me a cake as fast as you can.

Pat it, and dot it,

and mark it with a B,

And put it in the oven

For baby and me.

Name_____   Date/Story Number_____

Old Mister Rabbit

Old Mister Rabbit,

You've got a mighty habit,

Of jumping in my garden

And eating all my cabbage.

Name_____   Date/Story Number_____

Teddy Bear, Teddy Bear

Teddy Bear, Teddy Bear,
  turn around.

Teddy Bear, Teddy Bear,
  touch the ground.

Teddy Bear, Teddy Bear,
  turn out the lights.

Teddy Bear, Teddy Bear,
  say goodnight!

Name_____   Date/Story Number_____

Good Morning to You

Good morning to you

Good morning to you

Good morning dear _____

Good morning to you.

Name_____   Date/Story Number_____

Hop a Little, Jump a Little

Hop a little, jump a little,

One, two, three;

Run a little, skip a little,

Tap one knee;

Bend a little, stretch a little,

Nod your head;

Yawn a little, sleep a little,

In your bed.

Name _____   Date/Story Number_____

Hickory Dickory Dock

Hickory dickory dock,

The mouse ran up the clock!

The clock struck one.

The mouse ran down.

Hickory dickory dock.

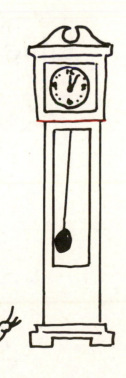

Name _____   Date/Story Number_____

Rain

Rain, rain, go away,

Come again some other day.

Little Rosie wants to play.

Lollipops

Lollipops, lollipops,

Lick, lick, lick.

Lollipops, lollipops,

Good on the stick.

Name_____   Date/Story Number_____

Soft Kitty

Soft kitty, warm kitty,

Little ball of fur.

Sleepy kitty, happy kitty,

Purr, purr, purrrrrrr.

Name _____   Date/Story Number_____

Jack and Jill

Jack and Jill went up the hill

To fetch a pail of water.

Jack fell down

And broke his crown.

And Jill came tumbling after.

Jack and Jill

Jack and Jill went up the hill

To fetch a pail of water.

Jack fell down and broke his crown.

And Jill came tumbling after.

Name _____   Date/Story Number_____

Fuzzy Wuzzy

Fuzzy Wuzzy

was a bear,

Fuzzy Wuzzy

had no hair,

Fuzzy Wuzzy

wasn't really fuzzy,

Was he?

Name_____   Date/Story Number_____

Valentines

Valentines red

Valentines blue

This valentine says

"I love you."

Name_____ Date _____ Number _____

Yo-Yo

I have a yellow yo-yo

And it can really go, go

You can try it.

Oh, no!

It wrapped around my toe, toe.

Letter Page (*B*)

148

Letter Page (C)

Letter Page (*D*)

Letter Page (F)

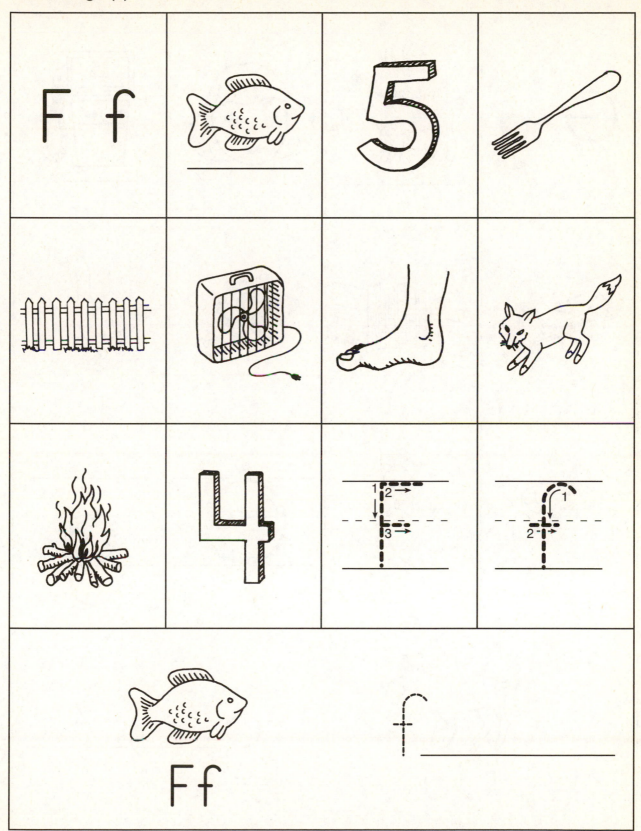

Letter Page (*G*)

Letter Page (*J*)

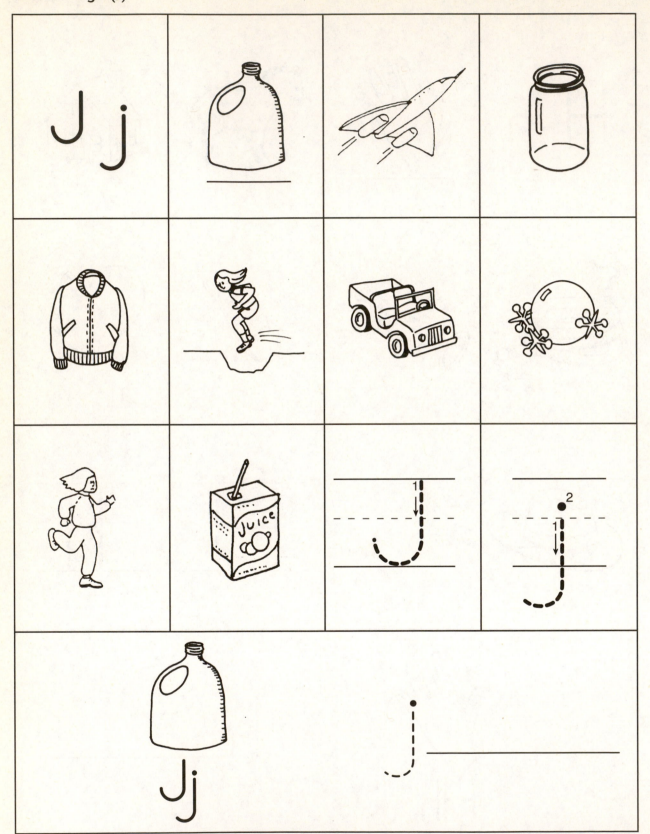

Letter Page (*K*)

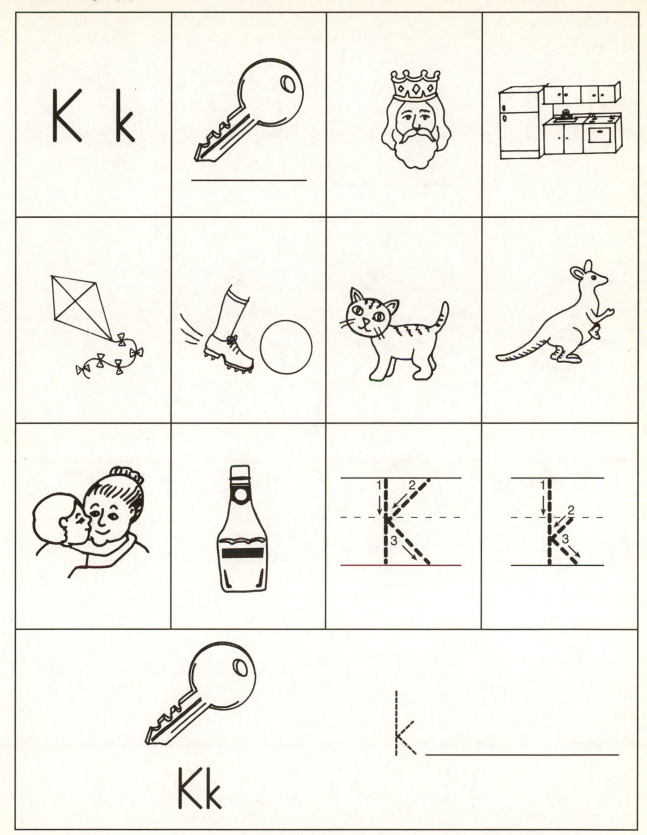

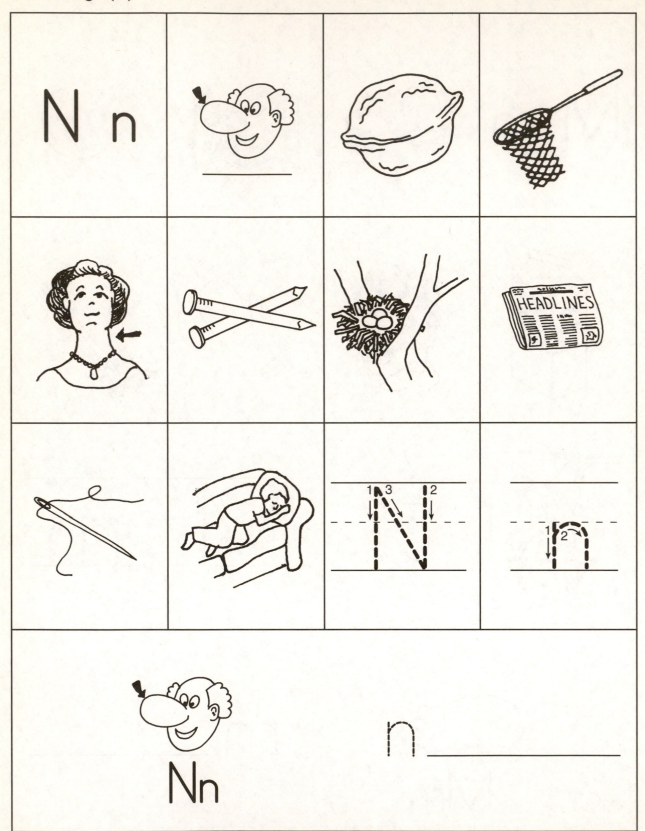

Letter Page (*P*)

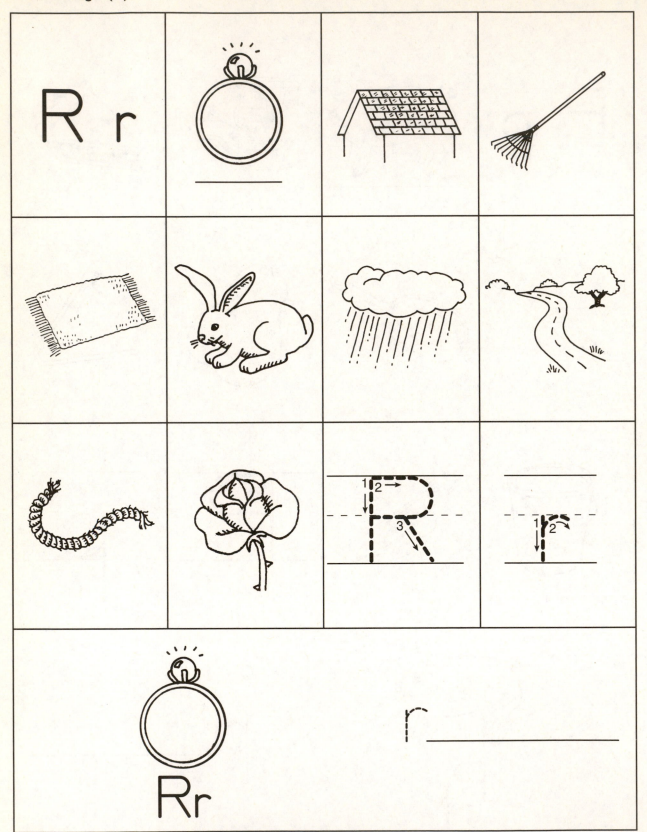

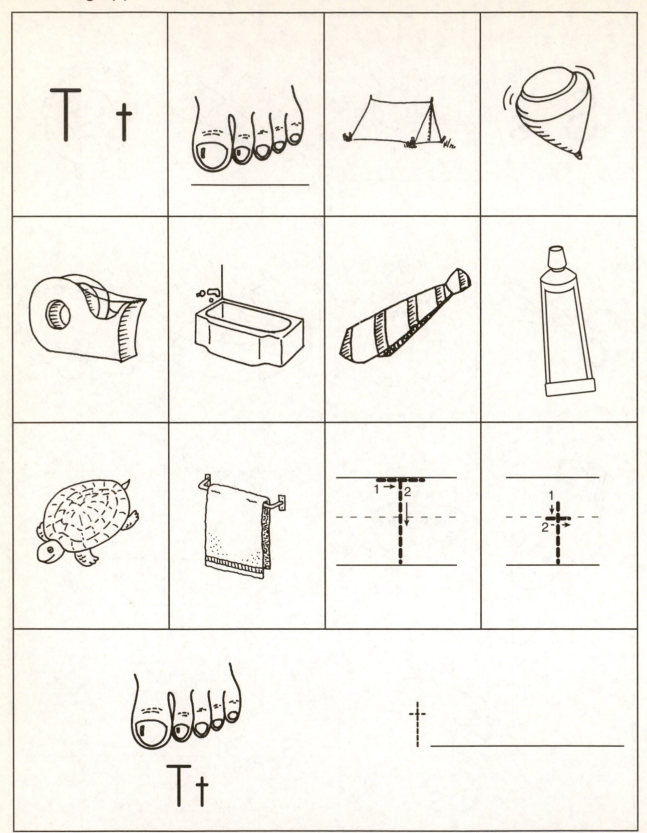

Letter Page (V)

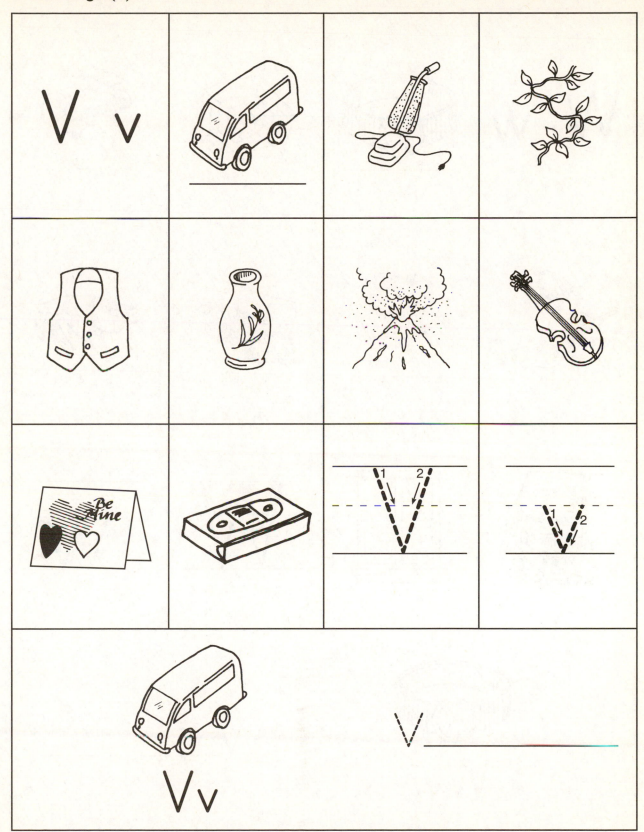

Letter Page (Y)

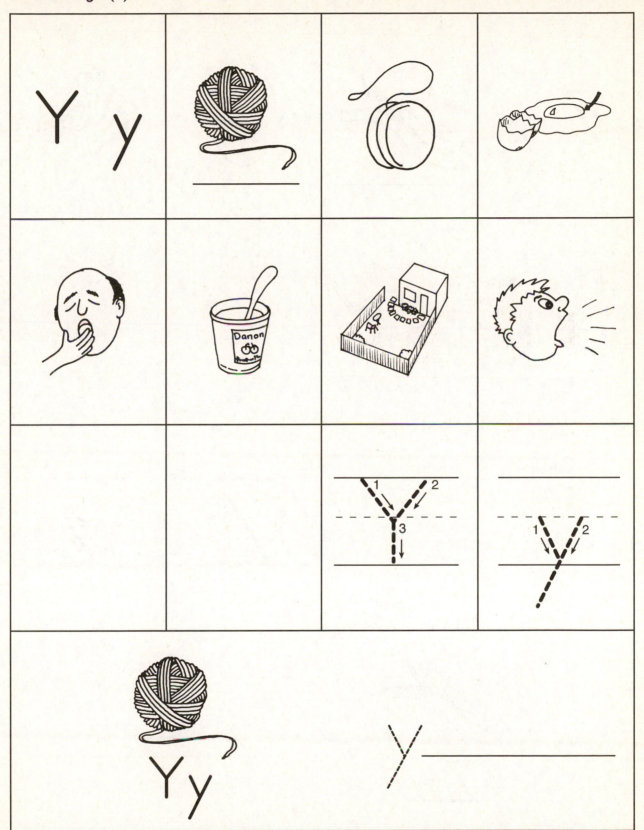

165

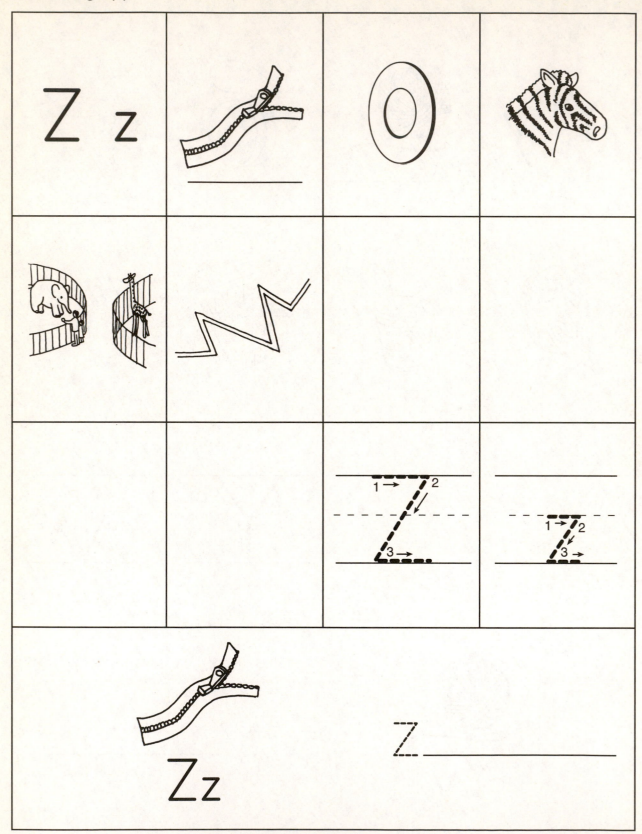

Chapter 6   Concept of Word in Print

NOTES FOR THE TEACHER

Background

Concept of word is the ability to accurately point to words as they are being read and depends on knowing how letters and sounds match up. Emergent learners do not have this skill and cannot read in the conventional sense. However, they can read with the support of simple memorable texts such as the eleven selections in this chapter and others throughout the book. Pointing to words as they reread familiar text is the best way for children to develop a concept of word and in the process they begin to read in a conventional way as they acquire sight words from repeated exposure. All parts of the literacy diet contribute to and benefit from concept of word. Additional information about concept of word and activities are presented in Chapters 4 and 5 of *Words Their Way*.

Targeted Learners

A concept of word assessment is provided in Chapter 1 and from that you should be able to identify where students are developmentally. The selections and activities in this chapter are designed for students in the middle to late emergent stage who lack a concept of word or have a rudimentary concept of word (can point but get off track). With some knowledge of the alphabet, some phonological awareness, and some consonant letter–sound matches these students begin to acquire a few sight words or words they can read from memory. They might build a sight vocabulary of perhaps 20 words through extensive repeated practice.

If students are able to track accurately and self-correct when they get off track they have a full concept of word. If they are also representing beginning and ending consonants in their spelling they are letter name–alphabet spellers and no longer emergent learners. They can still participate in group Read With activities but they do not need as much support and will benefit from reading text at their instructional level without having it read to them first. Students with a full concept of word are ready to acquire many words and benefit from the use of word banks and word walls.

Teaching Tips

There are eleven selections in this chapter as well as selections throughout this book that can be used in the same way. For all of them we have made suggestions about how to create integrated literacy lessons that include Read To, Read With, Write With, concept development, and word study for alphabet, phonological awareness, and beginning consonant sounds. The first two selections, *Rain on the Green Grass* and *Five Little Ducks*, are more fully developed than the others. We hope that these will serve as models for units you create yourself from your own favorite poems and reading materials.

Read With activities or shared reading are the starting point for developing concept of word. The teacher reads a selection aloud to students who choral read with the teacher; the students then read independently with their own copy of the selection. The word study activities you do as extensions to the reading selections should differ for students according to your assessment of their phonological awareness, alphabet knowledge, and knowledge of beginning sounds. Assessment is ongoing as you note how accurately students fingerpoint as they read. You can assess concept of word with any of these selections using the guidelines on page 26.

Personal Readers

Personal readers are collections of familiar reading selections that are stored in a notebook or folder to complement any reading program. Many selections are included ready to use in this book, but you can easily create others. Choose a selection that is three to eight lines long and type it in 26-point type or larger, leaving extra space between words and lines. Good fonts to use include Comic Sans MS and Century Gothic because the lower case *a* and *g* look like ɑ and ɡ. Number and date selections sequentially as they are added. Personal readers should also include storage for a word bank and a copy of the Words I Read form on page 179. You might also add a Sound Board for Consonants from Appendix B of *Words Their Way*.

Students in the emergent stage read the selections in their personal readers from memory, but through repetition and the activities suggested here, pretend reading gradually turns into real reading. Students learn to stay on track as they fingerpoint and begin to store words in their memory as sight words. Be sure parents understand that reading from memory is a way to support emergent readers (just like the hand they offered when children learned to walk), so they will be appreciative and excited when students bring their personal readers home to share.

STANDARD ROUTINES FOR CONCEPT OF WORD

1. *Read With.* Enlarge the text so that everyone in the group can easily see it, which can be done by creating an overhead, by printing the selection on a chart, or by creating sentence strips for a pocket chart. Text can come from songs (learn the song before reading the words in print), poems, nursery rhymes, finger plays, jingles, or other short and memorable selections of text. You can also do Read With activities using big books or you might read a longer book and enlarge only part of it to use for reading with emergent learners.

   Begin by reading the text to the children and then ask them to read along with you. In echo reading the teacher reads a line or a sentence and the students repeat it. In choral reading everyone reads along at the same time. On second and third readings you may want to slow down in order to point carefully to the print using a pointer such as an unsharpened pencil or dowel rod. Clap the syllables in longer words and show students how to touch them. Then invite children to take turns pointing to the words themselves, but more importantly, make individual copies of the selection so that children can fingerpoint for themselves. Individual copies can be placed in personal readers.

   During Read With lessons take the time to model and discuss concepts about print such as titles, left to right directionality, return sweep, punctuation, and capital and lowercase letters. Use terms like *beginning, end, sentence, word, syllable, rhyme, letter,* and so on, so children learn the terminology of literacy. Help children find rhyming words when appropriate.

2. *Sentence Strips and Cut-Up Sentences.* After working with the whole selection, focus on smaller parts such as sentences, words, and letters so that students examine

the print they have memorized. Most of the selections come with sentence strips that can be enlarged before copying, cut apart, and then matched back to the text. To demonstrate how to match, begin with a sentence from a familiar text and write it on a strip of tagboard. Show students how you match the strip back to the text. Reread the words to see if the sentence sounds the same. Sentence strips can also be cut into words. Students are then asked to rebuild the sentence by matching words back to a copy of the sentence or by memory. Students will need to consider at least the beginning sounds to get words in the right order.

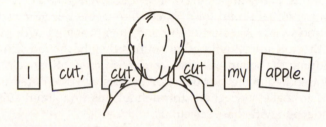

3. **Find Words and Letters.** Call out words or letters for all students to find either on the enlarged copy of the selection or on their own copies: "Can you find a capital *A*? How about a lowercase *a*? Find a word that starts with *b*. Find the word *fish*." They can simply point to the words and letters or they can underline or highlight them on their individual copies. When students have difficulty show them how to reread the sentence to find a word or prompt them with clues such as "What letter would *fffffish* start with?" Students can also work in pairs and call out words and letters for their partners to find.

Demonstrate how to underline familiar words in text: "I am going to point to words I know, words that I can read quickly, in a flash! If you read a word easily by itself, then underline the word." Show students how you make a line underneath a word using a pencil, crayon, or highlighter. Some students like to circle their choices though this is messy. Print out an extra copy for such underlining. Pieces of Wicki Sticks, translucent highlighting tape, or sticky notes can be used to underline words on enlarged copies. If you use a pocket chart you might want to use rectangles cut from colored plastic overheads to highlight words. Just tuck the plastic in the pocket over the word. To see how well these words are known in isolation, ask students to read the underlined words that you point to in random order.

4. **Collect Word Cards for Individual Word Banks.** Students who have a rudimentary concept of word can collect words from a selection to add to a word bank. (Consult Chapter 5 in *Words Their Way* for more information about developing and using word banks.) After students find words they know (they might underline them as described), and you have asked them to read the words, write the words on word cards. Use index cards, tagboard, or card stock to cut a supply of cards. One-by-three-inch cards are a good size. At the emergent stage there will not be many words to keep track of, so they can be stored easily in plastic bags or on a ring. Students who do not have a concept of word in print may not be able to collect sight words, so we can use this as an opportunity to ask them to identify letters. Have students say the letters they know as you write them on cards.

5. **Collect Words for Word Walls.** Many teachers have created alphabetic word walls to which high-frequency words are gradually added over time. In kindergarten the first words that go up are usually children's names. Later, one or two words at a time can be added from the selections used for Read With lessons. You should model how to use the word wall to find words you need to spell during Write With activities, reviewing

the words regularly. Keep in mind that for emergent learners the total number of high-frequency words should not be more than 20 to 30 words. It is helpful for emergent learners to have their own copy of the word wall words pasted in the front of their journal for easy reference during independent writing.

6. *Record Words I Read.* Record students' known words or letters on the *Words I Read* form on page 179 and keep this in their personal readers. There is a place to log the date of the entries. To make it easier to return to context, number the selections in students' personal readers and record the story number.

7. *Word Study for Beginning Consonants.* The reading selections that follow can be used as a starting point or follow-up for word study activities that focus on initial consonant sounds. For example, the first selection, *Rain on the Green Grass*, is a natural link with the initial sound for *r*. After reading the selections students can first be asked to find words that start with *r* and then provided with pictures of things that start with *r* to contrast with other sounds they have studied in a picture sort. Or, after studying the sound of *r*, they can revisit the familiar selection to hunt for words. Although beginning consonants were described in detail in Chapter 5, we will continue to make suggestions throughout this unit about suitable consonant study in connection with these selections.

RAIN ON THE GREEN GRASS

Read To and Talk With

This is a great poem to introduce on a rainy day (see page 180). You might start by sharing the wordless book *Rain* by Peter Spiers and encourage children to talk about what they see in the pictures. (The illustrations are rather small so leave the book out for children to look at on their own and revisit at another time to talk about more of the details they are likely to notice). Ask children about their own experiences in the rain. Explain that they are going to learn a poem about rain.

Read With: *Rain on the Green Grass*

Bring in an umbrella (*paraguas* in Spanish—similar to *parasol*) and talk about what it is used for and other ways to keep dry in the rain. Enlarge the pictures on page 180 and use them to orally introduce children to *Rain on the Green Grass*. Hold up a picture for each line and then repeat in an echo fashion. Say the line and have students repeat after you, adding simple hand movements. Let children take turns holding the umbrella and saying the last line. Use the pictures to teach vocabulary to your ELs by pointing to the rain and then the objects named in the poem. Create an enlarged copy of the text so all the students in your group can see the print, and as you read each line put the matching picture beside it. Reread the poem several times while you model pointing and ask children to join in. Give each student a copy to practice pointing.

Rain on the Green Grass

Rain on the green grass,
Rain on the tree,
Rain on the housetop,
But not on me!

Work with Sentences and Words

Create sentence strips for each line of the poem (page 181) and rebuild the poem as described in the ongoing routines on pages 168–169. Give children a second copy of the poem that they can cut apart and rebuild the same way, placing each line beside a

Literature Connection

Arnosky, J. (1997). *Rabbits and raindrops.* New York: Putnam.

Hesse, K., & Muth, J. J. (1999). *Come on, rain!* New York: Scholastic.

Hoban, J. (1989). *Amy loves the rain.* New York: HarperCollins.

Yashimo, T. (1958). *Umbrella.* New York: Viking.

picture. Save the pieces to repeat on a second or third day and then supply paper so that students can paste it down.

Word Study

Phonological Awareness

Ask students to find the words that rhyme.

Sight Words

There are a number of high-frequency words in this poem that are good choices to teach as sight words to students in the middle to late emergent stage: *on, the, green, and, not,* and *me.* Write the words on cards, hold up each one, and ask students to find it on the enlarged copy and on their own copies of the poem. Then say each word without showing it. Ask students what they need to look for to find the word *me*—it starts with an *M*! Select some words to add to the class word wall and to individual word banks. Students may self-select more concrete words for their word bank, such as *rain* or *grass.*

Read To

Share other books about rainy day adventures such as the ones listed above.

Talk With and Write With

Talk with the students about their experiences in the rain and with umbrellas and then have them dictate sentences for you to record. A frame sentence might work well with ELs, such as "I like to _____ in the rain."

Concept Sort 21: Wet and Dry

An umbrella will keep you dry in the rain. Brainstorm with children other things that they use to keep dry in the rain. Enlarge a copy of the concept sort for wet and dry on page 182 and display the pictures. After naming all the pictures, ask students to find things that will keep them dry and things that will not. See other ideas for concept sorts in Chapter 2.

Extend

Two other selections in this book feature rain—*Rain* on page 140 and *Raining* on page 183. Either or both can be presented as just described under Read With. Sentence strips for *Raining* on page 184 can be used similarly to the previous example.

FIVE LITTLE DUCKS

Five Little Ducks is a traditional song that has been made into many picture book versions. You can teach the song without the book but *Five Little Ducks* illustrated by Paparone or by Raffi are fun to share before or after learning the song. A great source for songs, http://bussongs.com, can be accessed if you don't know all the words.

Literature Connection

Briers, E., & Boey, S. (2004). *Little duck lost.* New York: Dutton Juvenile.

Dunn, J. (1976). *The little duck.* New York: Random House.

Ginsburg, M. (1988). *The chick and the duckling.* London: Aladdin Library.

Paprone, P. (1997). *Five little ducks.* New York: North-South Books.

Raffi. (1992). *Five little ducks.* New York: Crown Books.

Root, P., & Chapman, J. (2003). *One duck stuck.* Cambridge, MA: Candlewick..

Read With

Make an enlarged copy of the first verse (see page 185) or write the words on sentence strips (see page 186). Make a copy for each student. Model how to point to the words as you sing, but then say the words more slowly so students can follow on their own copies. You can also make word cards for numbers four, three, two, and one, as well as words and phrases from other verses, substituting them to recreate the other verses.

Five Little Ducks

Five little ducks went out one day.
Over the hills and far away.
Mother duck said, "Quack, quack, quack, quack."
But only four little ducks came back.

Work with Sentence Strips and Word Cards

Create sentence strips for each line of the poem and use them to rebuild the story. Give children a second copy of the poem (page 185) that they can cut apart and rebuild in the same way, placing each line beside a picture. Make another sentence strip of the first line ("Five little ducks went out one day") and cut it into word cards. Hold up words in a random order and ask students to find them in the text. Repeat without showing the word. Ask students what they need to look for to find the word *duck*—it starts with a *d*! Rebuild the sentence as a group and then make a strip for each child to cut apart and rebuild. They can paste it down and draw a picture to go with it.

Consonant Sort 22: *F, D, & H*

Prepare a copy of the beginning consonant sort for *F, D, H* and enlarge it for modeling (see page 187). Make word cards for *five, far, ducks, day,* and *hills.* Hold up the letter *F* and ask students to find words in the rhyme that start with capital *F* and lowercase *f* (*Five, far*). In a pocket chart or on a flat surface put the word *Five* under the letter card for *F*. Explain, "*Five* and *far* both begin with the /ffff/ sound (point to the first letter in the word), so I will put them under the letter *F*." Repeat with *D* (*ducks, day*) and *H* (*hills*). Then display all the other pictures and name them with the students. Provide extra support for your ELs, asking them to say each word after you. Select three pictures and model how to name the picture, listen for the first sound, and sort it under the letter that goes with that sound. Then ask students to help you sort the rest of the pictures.

Sort, Check, and Reflect

After sorting, name all the pictures in each column, emphasizing the first sound. Repeat the sort as a group and check each column by naming the pictures and moving any that are wrong. Ask the students how the pictures in each column are alike. Make a copy of the sort for individual children or put the sort in a center where children can sort it again independently. See the list of weekly routines in Chapter 5.

Extend

There are a number of high-frequency words in this song that are good choices to teach as sight words to students in the late emergent stage, including the number words. Select two or three words to add to the class word wall. Harvest words for a word bank as described on page 169.

Read To

There are lots of books about ducks to read aloud. *The Little Duck* by Dunn offers information about real ducks through colorful photographs and can be compared to other books in a discussion of real and make believe. See the concept sort on page 133 that goes with *Hey Diddle Diddle*.

Talk With and Write With

Ask the students what they think the little ducks were doing while they were away from their mother. Encourage them to think of lots of possibilities. Their ideas can be recorded as dictations or you can ask them to write their own ideas, spelling as best they can.

THE REMAINING SELECTIONS

Peas Porridge

Introduce this poem (see page 188) by explaining to students that porridge is like oatmeal. Use the standard routines given earlier in this chapter for reading together and memorizing the rhyme. Students enjoy changing their faces as they attempt to taste the porridge: *hot, cold,* and a yucky *nine days old!*

Peas Porridge

Peas porridge hot,	Some like it hot,
Peas porridge cold,	Some like it cold,
Peas porridge in the pot	Some like it in the pot
Nine days old.	Nine days old!

Write the second stanza on a pocket chart or as a writing frame with blanks and have students substitute cards for key words:

Substitute names for *Some: Rodney likes it hot*
Substitute temperatures for *hot: Some like it freezing*
Substitute numbers for *Nine: Seven days old*

Give students copies of the sentence strips on page 189 and have them rebuild the second stanza of the rhyme. They can use the number cards to substitute for *nine*.

Word Study

Phonological Awareness.   Ask students to find the words that rhyme. Brainstorm other words that rhyme with *hot/pot* or *old/cold*.

Beginning Consonants.   Ask students for words that start with *p* (*peas, porridge, pot*), *h* (*hot*), *l* (*like*), and *n* (*nine*). Sort pictures that begin with these sounds as described in

Chapter 5. Use only two contrasting letters with students just getting started in the study of consonant sounds, perhaps focusing on just *p* and *n*.

Sight Words. The word *like* is a good sight word for students to learn and the sentence frame *I like* _____ can be the beginning of many dictated or independently written sentences. Students can fill in foods that they like to eat and then illustrate the sentence.

Jump Rope

Students chant as they pretend to jump rope and will enjoy the chant on the playground as they jump rope (see page 190). Use the standard routines on page 168 for reading together and memorizing the rhyme. Point out the question mark and exclamation mark and model how to interpret the punctuation. Show students how the voice rises at the question mark and how the final line is read with excitement.

Jump Rope

Jump rope, jump rope,
Will I miss?
Jump rope, jump rope,
Just watch this!

Word Study

Ask students to find the words that rhyme. Ask students to find words that start with *j* (*jump, just*), *r* (*rope*), *w* (*will, watch*), and *m* (*miss*). Sort pictures that begin with these sounds as a follow-up.

Extend

Teddy Bear is a jump rope chant you can find on page 136. It can be used in connection with this rhyme. Other jump rope rhymes can be found in a number of books, including JoAnna Cole's *Anna Banana: 101 Jump Rope Rhymes*.

On the Bed

Before introducing this selection read aloud one or more of the books listed in the Literature Connection. This cumulative story on page 192 has pictures to match to the side of each line. Use the standard routines on page 168 for reading together and memorizing the rhyme. Students use the word cards on the blackline on page 193 to match underneath the first line of the rhyme. They may need some guidance as they attempt to point to the two-syllable words.

On the Bed

My mama sits on the bed.
My papa sits on the bed.
My sister sits on the bed.
My dog sits on the bed.

In a small group, use frame sentences in a pocket chart to substitute words that come to mind. Ask students to tell you an animal that sits on the bed whose name begins with the /c/ sound: "My *cat* sits on the bed." Students can call out their own substitutions: "My *grandmother* sits on the bed." Other words can be substituted for *sits:* "My sister *jumps* on the bed."

Students can make up their own verses that can be typed in 26-point text and placed in their personal readers. For example, students can use different verbs instead of *sits:* "My mama sings with me. My papa dances with me. My sister runs with me." Students

Literature Connection

Christalow, E. (1999). *Five little monkeys jumping on the bed.* Boston: Clarion.

Peek, M. (1981). *Roll over: A country song.* Boston: Houghton Mifflin.

Wood, A. (1984). *The napping house.* New York: Harcourt.

like to act out and then read about animals and their movements: "My monkey climbs on the bed. My monkey jumps on the bed."

Word Study

Ask students for words that start with *m* (*my*), *f* (*family*), *b* (*bed*), *s* (*sits, sister*), and so on. Sort pictures that begin with these sounds as a follow-up to the concept of word activities described in Chapter 5.

English Language Learners

English language learners may read a translation more easily. For example:

Mi familia se sienta en la cama

Mi mama se sienta en la cama.
Mi papa se sienta en la cama.
Mi hermana se sienta en la cama.
Mi perro se sienta en la cama.

Row, Row, Row Your Boat

Row, Row, Row Your Boat is a well-known song (see page 194), so begin by singing it. Then use the standard routines on page 168 for reading together and memorizing the rhyme. The single-syllable words in the first line make this selection easy for early emergent readers to track. Model how to track *gently* in the second line and *Merrily* on the third line and observe which children are able to stay on track. To find their way, students should use their knowledge of the letter *m* to track from one *merrily* to the next.

Row, Row, Row Your Boat

Row, row, row your boat
Gently down the stream.
Merrily, merrily, merrily, merrily,
Life is but a dream.

Word Study

Ask students to find the words that rhyme. Ask students for words that start with *r* (*row*), *b* (*boat, but*), *l* (*life*), *m* (*merrily*), and so on. Sort pictures that begin with these sounds as a follow-up to the concept of word activities.

Extend

Substitute different movements for different forms of transportation:

Dance, dance, dance your feet
Ride, ride, ride your bike
Drive, drive, drive your car
All the way to the movies/baseball game/school/Sarah's house

Literature Connection

Crew, D. (1995). *Ten black dots.* New York: HarperTrophy.

DK Publishing. (2002). *My first Spanish number board book.* New York: DK Preschool.

Walsh, E. S. (1995). *Mouse count.* New York: Voyager Books.

One, Two, Buckle My Shoe

The numbers and rhythm of this rhyme, shown on page 195, make it a fun one to track, and there are lots of ways to tie this into math. Use the standard routines on page 168 for reading together and memorizing the rhyme. Students can be asked to hold up the correct number of fingers as they recite the rhyme and add motions for the various actions. Students may not know the meaning of the word *buckle.* You might find a pair of sandals that buckle to show them.

Students can also sort the pictures to the right of each line using the sentence strips on page 196. They can refer to first words only to put the strips in order from smallest to largest number.

Concept Sort: Shoes

Sort students' shoes by the way they fasten: laces, Velcro, slip-ons, and so on, and label the categories after sorting to reinforce the vocabulary.

Rhyme Sort 23

Rhyming Words.   Ask students to find the words that rhyme. Brainstorm more words that rhyme with *two/shoe, four/door, six/sticks, eight/straight,* and *ten/hen.* Follow up with the rhyme sort on page 197.

2	3	5	6
8	10	key	hen
chicks	men	zoo	gate
drive	bee	skate	sticks
shoe	plate	tree	hive
pea	dive	glue	bricks

Beginning Sounds.   Ask students for words that start with *t* (*two, ten*), *b* (*buckle, big*), *f* (*four, five, fat*), *h* (*hen*), and so on. Sort pictures that begin with these sounds as a follow-up.

Extend

Teach students to count in Spanish up to five: *uno, dos, tres, cuatro, cinco.* Find out how to count up to five in the other languages you may have represented in your class.

Show students how to play Pick Up Sticks as they learn this rhyme. They can be asked to pick up the number you call out: "Pick up two sticks, now four," and so on.

Happy Birthday

The familiar song *Happy Birthday* is celebratory (see page 198) and can be used whenever a child has a birthday. Use the standard routines for reading together and memorizing the rhyme. The two-syllable words offer a challenge in pointing for early emergent readers. Sing *Happy Birthday* and track the song on a chart. A pocket chart makes it easy to add students' names. Make a word card of the student's name to add to the end of the third line and have children draw candles on the cake. When it is a student's birthday, give the student a special copy of this page with his or her name written in special writing in a bold color or gold marker.

Happy Birthday

Happy Birthday to you,
Happy Birthday to you,
Happy Birthday dear _____,
Happy Birthday to you.

Word Study

Ask students for words that start with *h* (*happy*), *b* (*birthday*), *d* (*dear*), *t* (*to*), or *y* (*you*). Sort pictures that begin with these sounds as a follow-up to the concept of word activities.

Sound Play

Some students like to play a sound game in which they substitute a different sound at the beginning of the words: "*Pappy Pirthday, Dappy Dirthday,*" and so on.

Extend

Investigate the birthday traditions of other cultures represented in your room. For example, piñatas are often used in Mexico and have become popular in the United States as well. Some books about birthdays are listed below to read aloud.

Rags

Dogs are always a favorite topic and this rhyme offers some good imagery (see page 199). Use the standard routines for reading together and memorizing the rhyme. Children will be eager to talk about dogs they have known. Take dictations or encourage students to write about and illustrate their own ideas.

Rags

I have a dog. His name is Rags.
He eats so much his tummy sags.
His ears flip flop and his tail wig wags.
And when he walks he goes zig-zag.

Literature Connection

Hill, E. (1981). *Spot's birthday*. New York: Putnam.

Hutchins, P. (1978). *Happy birthday Sam*. New York: Greenwillow.

Keats, E. J. (1968). *A letter to Amy*. New York: HarperCollins.

Peek, M. (1985). *Mary wore her red dress and Henry wore his green sneakers*. Boston: Clarion.

Rice, E. (1981). *Benny bakes a cake*. New York: Greenwillow.

Literature Connection

Aliki. (1999). *My visit to the zoo.* New York: HarperCollins.

Campbell, R. (1972). *Dear zoo.* London: Campbell Books.

Carle, E. (1996). *1, 2, 3 to the zoo.* New York: Putnam & Grosset.

Paxton, T., & Schmidt, K. (1996). *Going to the zoo.* New York: HarperCollins.

Rathman, P. (1996). *Goodnight gorilla.* New York: Putnam Juvenile.

Word Study

Find rhyming words. Find words that start with *d* (*dog*), *t* (*tail*), *w* (*wig wag*), and *z* (*zig-zag*). Sort pictures that begin with these sounds as a follow-up to the concept of word activities.

Zoo

Share books about going to the zoo listed above. Use the standard routines on page 168 for reading together and memorizing the rhyme on page 201.

> ### Zoo
>
> Let's go to the zoo.
> You can come too.
> We like the zebra.
> And the kangaroo.

Word Study

This is particularly good to use for introducing the sound for *z* (*zoo, zebra*).

Words I Read

Words			Reads		
Date	Story Number		Date	Story Number	

Name_____ Date _____ Number _____

Rain on the Green Grass

Rain on the green grass,

Rain on the tree,

Rain on the housetop,

But not on me!

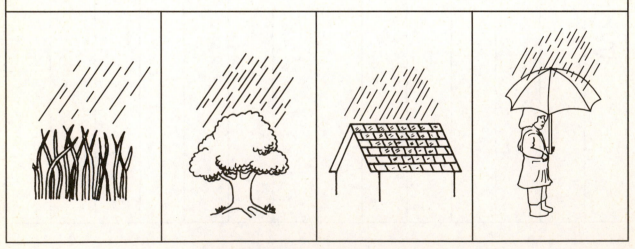

Rain on the Green Grass

Rain on the green grass,

Rain on the tree,

Rain on the housetop,

But not on me!

SORT 21   Concept Sort for Wet and Dry

Name_____ Date _____ Number _____

Raining

It's raining, it's pouring,

The old man is snoring.

He went to bed and bumped his head,

And couldn't get up in the morning.

Raining

It's raining, it's pouring,

The old man is snoring.

He went to bed and bumped his head,

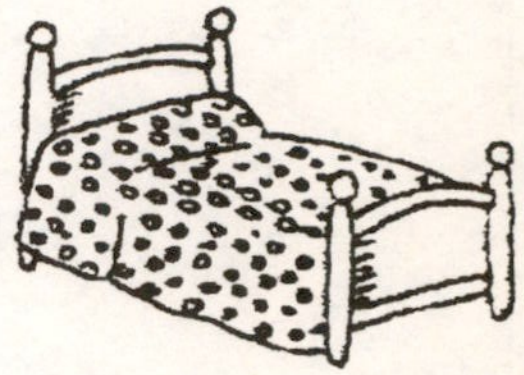

And couldn't get up in the morning.

Name_____ Date _____ Number _____

Five Little Ducks

Five little ducks went out one day

Over the hills and far away

Mother duck said,

quack, quack, quack, quack,

But only four little ducks came back.

Five Little Ducks

Five little ducks went out one day

Over the hills and far away

Mother duck said,

quack, quack, quack, quack,

But only four little ducks came back.

SORT 22 Beginning Consonant Sort for *F, D, & H*

Name_____   Date/Story Number_____

Peas Porridge Hot

Peas porridge hot,

Peas porridge cold,

Peas porridge in the pot

Nine days old.

Some like it hot,

Some like it cold,

Some like it in the pot

Nine days old!

Some like it hot,

Some like it cold,

Some like it the pot,

Nine days old.

One	Two	Three	Four	Five
Six	Ten	Seven	Eight	Nine

Name_____   Date/Story Number_____

Jump Rope

Jump rope, jump rope,

Will I miss?

Jump rope, jump rope,

Just watch this!

Jump Rope

Jump rope, jump rope,

Will I miss?

Jump rope, jump rope,

Just watch this!

Name _____ Date _____ Number _____

On the Bed

My mama sits on the bed.

My papa sits on the bed.

My sister sits on the bed.

My dog sits on the bed.

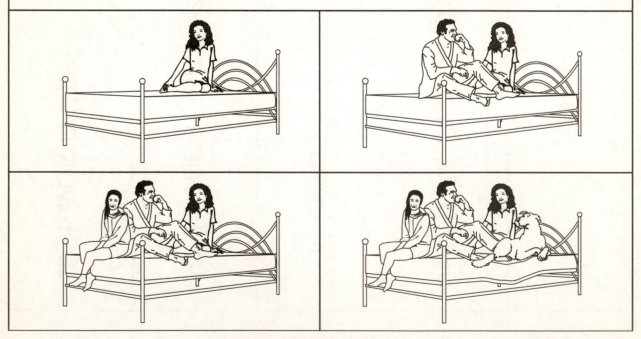

Word Cards for *On the Bed*

My mama sits on the bed.	My	I	the
	sits	dog	bed
	on	cat	sit
	sister	papa	mother
	mama	daddy	brother

Name _____   Date/Story Number_____

Row, Row, Row Your Boat

Row, row, row your boat

Gently down the stream.

Merrily, merrily, merrily, merrily,

Life is but a dream.

Name_____   Date/Story Number_____

One, Two, Buckle My Shoe

One, two, buckle my shoe,

Three, four, shut the door.

Five, six, pick up sticks.

Seven, eight, lay them straight.

Nine, ten, a big fat hen.

One, Two, Buckle My Shoe

One, two, buckle my shoe,

Three, four, shut the door.

Five, six, pick up sticks.

Seven, eight, lay them straight.

Nine, ten, a big fat hen.

SORT 23   Rhyming Sort with Numbers

Name_____   Date/Story Number_____

Happy Birthday

Happy Birthday to you,

Happy Birthday to you,

Happy Birthday dear _____,

Happy Birthday to you.

Name_____   Date/Story Number_____

Rags

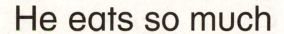

I have a dog.

His name is Rags.

He eats so much

His tummy sags.

His ears flip flop

And his tail wig wags.

And when he walks

He goes zig-zag.

Rags

I have a dog. His name is Rags.

He eats so much his tummy sags.

His ears flip flop and his tail wig wags.

And when he walks he goes zig-zag.

Name_____   Date/Story Number_____

Zoo

Let's go to the zoo.

You can come too.

We like the zebra.

And the kangaroo.

Zoo

Let's go to the zoo.

You can come too.

We like the zebra.

And the kangaroo.

Appendix

Blank Template for Picture Sorts 3 × 4

Blank Template for Picture Sorts 3 × 5

Blank Template for Word Sorts 4 × 5

Blank Template for Word Sorts 4 × 6

List of Pictures on Letter Pages

Blank Template for Picture Sorts 3 × 4

Blank Template for Picture Sorts 3 × 5

Blank Template for Word Sorts 4 × 5

Appendix

Blank Template for Word Sorts 4 × 6

Appendix

List of Pictures on Letter Pages

Appendix

B	C	D	F	G
boy	cat	dog	fish	goat
bed	cup	deer	five	girl
belt	cow	doll	fork	gas
bat	cake	duck	fence	gum
bird	coat	door	fan	gate
book	car	desk	foot	game
boat	corn	dice	fox	goose
bug	comb	dive	fire	gold
bear	can	dishes	four	ghost

H	J	K	L	M
hand	jug	key	lamp	mouse
horse	jet	king	leaf	map
house	jar	kitchen	log	moon
hose	jacket	kite	lock	milk
horn	jump	kick	letter	man
hook	jeep	kitten	leg	mitten
heart	jacks	kangaroo	lips	mop
hat	jog	kiss	lake	monkey
hill	juice	ketchup	lion	mask

N	P	R	S	T
nose	pig	ring	sun	toes
nut	paint	roof	saw	tent
net	pie	rake	sad	top
neck	pen	rug	scissors	tape
nails	pan	rabbit	sack	tub
nest	pear	rain	sink	tie
newspaper	pin	road	soap	tube
needle	pail	rope	socks	turtle
nap	peas	rose	soup	towel

V	W	Y	Z
van	watch	yarn	zipper
vacuum	web	yo-yo	zero
vine	worm	yolk	zebra
vest	witch	yawn	zoo
vase	wig	yogurt	zig-zag
volcano	wall	yard	
violin	wing	yell	
valentine	well		
videotape	window		